THE BIRD ATLAS

Illustrated by Richard Orr
Written by Barbara Taylor

DK

DORLING KINDERSLEY
London • New York • Stuttgart

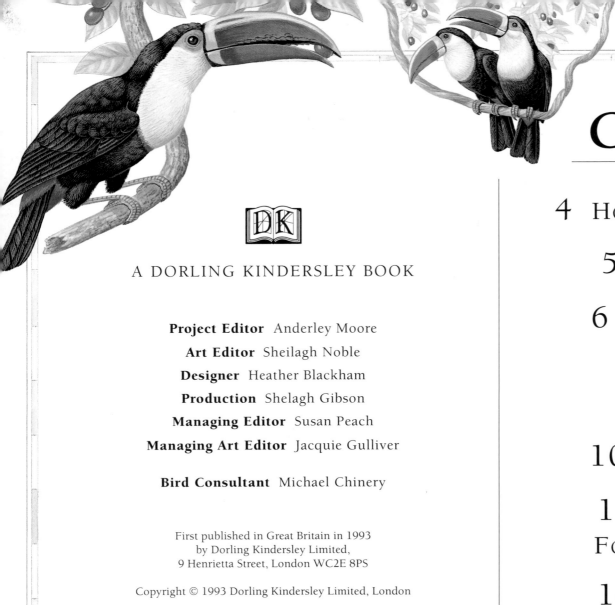

DK

A DORLING KINDERSLEY BOOK

Project Editor Anderley Moore
Art Editor Sheilagh Noble
Designer Heather Blackham
Production Shelagh Gibson
Managing Editor Susan Peach
Managing Art Editor Jacquie Gulliver

Bird Consultant Michael Chinery

First published in Great Britain in 1993
by Dorling Kindersley Limited,
9 Henrietta Street, London WC2E 8PS

A CIP catalogue record for this book is available
from the British Library.

ISBN - 0-7513-5068-0

Reproduced in Hong Kong by Bright Arts
Printed in Italy by New Interlitho, Milan

CONTENTS

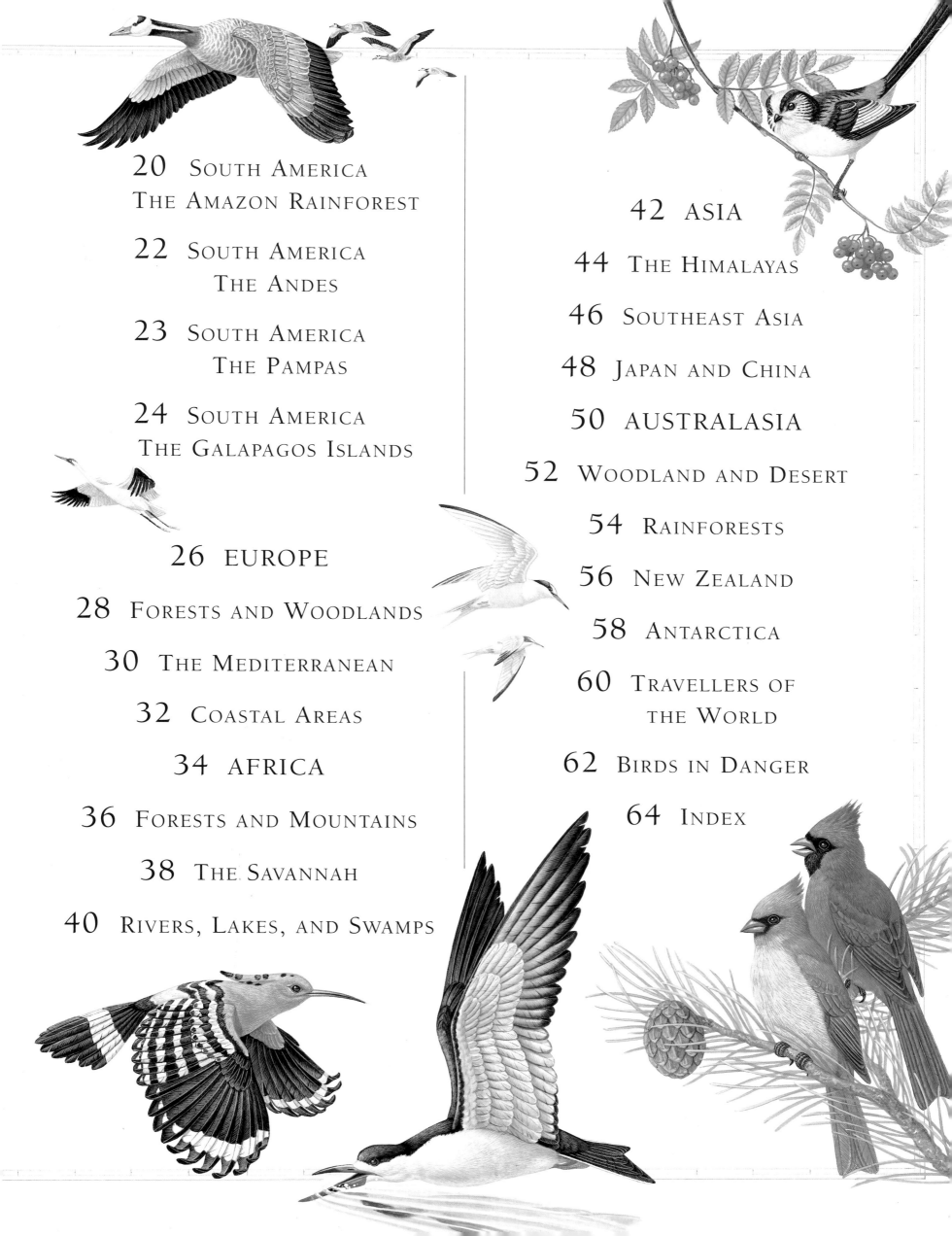

How to Use This Atlas

THE BIRD ATLAS IS ARRANGED in order of continent – the Americas, Europe, Africa, Asia, Australia, and Antarctica. A double-page, such as the one on Africa (right), introduces the continent as a whole. This is followed by pages showing the main places where birds live – their habitats – within that continent.

When turning to any page you can see which continent it is about by looking at the heading in the top left-hand corner; the habitat featured is given in the top right-hand corner. The sample pages here show how the information is presented on the two main types of pages – continental and habitat pages – and explain the maps, symbols, and abbreviations used.

CONTINENTAL PAGES

These pages introduce the continent and give an overview of the climate, landscape, main bird habitats, typical birds, and amazing birds to be found there. A large map shows the size of the continent, its position on the globe, and major geographical features. There is also usually a feature on how the position of the continent has changed over millions of years as a result of continental drift.

WHERE ON EARTH?

The red shaded area on this globe shows the location of the habitat featured on the page. For example, the shaded area on this globe shows the position of Central America and the Caribbean within the Americas.

BIRD SYMBOLS

Symbols of each of the birds illustrated on the page show the main areas where each species lives, although some birds live all over the region. By looking at the key, you can identify the birds and then find them on the map.

Length: 30 cm
(12 in)

HOW BIG?

Labels next to each bird tell you how big it is. The length of a bird is measured from the tip of the bill to the end of the tail. Sometimes male and female birds look different from one another and are very different in size. In these cases, measurements for males and females are given separately. In special cases, the wingspan, length of tail feathers, or height of the bird may also be given. For example, on this page you can find out how big a quetzal is and also discover the length of the male's remarkable tail feathers.

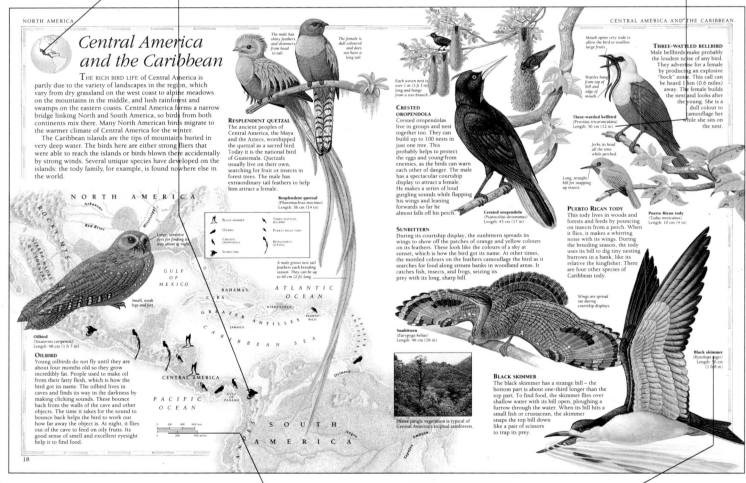

SCALE

You can use this scale to work out the size of the area shown on the map.

Black skimmer
Rhynchops niger

LATIN NAMES

Scientists have given each species of bird a Latin name. This means that people from all over the world can use the same name to identify birds, no matter what language they speak. A bird's Latin name is divided into two parts. The first name is a group name given to a number of similar birds. For example, *Rhynchops* is the group name for skimmers. The second part of the name identifies the particular species of bird and often tells you something more specific about it. In this case it is *niger*, the Latin word for black.

ABBREVIATIONS USED IN THE ATLAS:			
Metric		**Imperial**	
mm	millimetre	in	inch
cm	centimetre	ft	foot
m	metre	mph	miles per hour
km	kilometre	sq miles	square miles
sq km	square kilometres	lb	pound
kph	kilometres per hour	F	fahrenheit
kg	kilogram		
C	centigrade		

What is a Bird?

BIRDS ARE THE ONLY ANIMALS in the world that have feathers. They also lay eggs, breathe air, and keep their body temperature the same all the time. This is called being warm-blooded. Birds developed or evolved from reptiles about 150 million years ago. The earliest bird we know of, *Archaeopteryx* (meaning ancient wing), lived at this time. It was about the size of a crow and had feathers, although it probably couldn't fly very well. From early birds like *Archaeopteryx*, the 9,000 or so species of bird alive today have developed.

Archaeopteryx

Body or contour feather from a red lory.

Down feather from a pigeon.

Flight feather from a Guinea fowl.

FEATHERS

A bird has a vast number of feathers. Even a small bird, such as a wren, has more than 1,000 feathers. There are three main types of feather – flight feathers on the wings and tail, body feathers to cover the body and give a bird its shape, and fluffy down feathers to keep it warm. Flight feathers are made of strands called barbs which hook together. If the hooks come apart, they can be drawn together again, rather like doing up a zip. Each year, a bird sheds or moults most of its feathers and grows new ones to replace them.

A bird's wing is light, strong, and flexible so it will not snap as the bird twists and turns through the air.

Peregrine falcon
(*Falco peregrinus*)

The bill is lightweight, but very strong; birds do not have teeth.

Pigeon
(*Columba livia*)

BIRD BONES

A bird has a bony skeleton inside its body to support and protect delicate organs, such as its heart, lungs, and brain. But the whole skeleton of flying birds is very light and the long bones in their wings and legs are hollow, with a honeycomb of stiff supporting struts (above). This means they have less weight to lift off the ground and keep up in the air.

A bird uses its tail feathers for steering as it flies through the air.

Birds have scaly legs like their reptile ancestors.

Pigeons and many other birds have a flapping flight. Others, such as eagles and albatrosses glide long distances without flapping their wings much at all. Hummingbirds can even hover.

HOW BIRDS FLY

Birds are the largest, fastest, and most powerful flying animals alive. They have a smooth, streamlined shape to cut through the air easily, their front limbs are wings to push them along, and they have powerful chest muscles to help them flap their wings up and down. A bird's wings are curved on top and flat underneath. As a bird flies, this aerofoil shape creates an area of high air pressure under the wing and an area of low air pressure above it. The high pressure under the wing pushes the bird up into the air. Some birds, such as penguins and ostriches, cannot fly; they run or swim very fast instead.

BIRD BILLS

Birds use their bills to catch and hold their food, care for their feathers, and build nests. The size and shape of a bird's bill depends on what it eats and where it finds its food.

Pine grosbeak
(*Pinicola enucleator*)
Seed-eater

Small green barbet
(*Megalaima viridis*)
Fruit and insect-eater

African paradise flycatcher
(*Terpsiphone viridis*)
Insect-eater

Australian darter
(*Anhinga novaehollandiae*)
Fish-eater

EGGS AND CHICKS

All birds lay eggs. The hard eggshell protects the developing chick and there is a food store inside the egg. Air can pass through the eggshell to reach the developing chick inside. The chick also has a food store inside the egg. While the chick develops, the parents have to keep the eggs warm by sitting on them. This is called incubation. Many birds are blind, featherless, and helpless when they hatch out. Other birds, such as this duckling, spend longer inside the egg and so are better developed when they hatch out. They can run about and fend for themselves almost as soon as they hatch.

A duckling starts to break out of its shell by cutting a circle with its bill.

When the young bird pushes itself out of the shell its feathers are still wet.

Within three hours its feathers are dry and fluffy and it can run around.

Where Birds Live

BIRDS LIVE IN EVERY CORNER OF the globe. They have spread so far because they can fly from one place to another, live on a variety of foods, and maintain a constant body temperature in most weathers.

The place where a bird lives is called its habitat. This is rather like its "home address". A bird's habitat must provide food, shelter, and somewhere to nest. Some birds, such as the barn owl, can live in a range of habitats from woodland to scrub; others are more specialized (toucans, for example, live only in the rainforests of Central and South America). Some birds stay permanently in one habitat, while others move away – migrate – at certain times of year. As well as natural habitats, there are an increasing number of man-made habitats, such as houses, parks, and gardens. Some of the most common birds are those that have adapted to live in these new habitats near people, such as starlings and sparrows.

The main types of bird habitat around the world are shown at the bottom of these pages.

LOOK-ALIKES

Birds have developed in different ways according to the habitat in which they live and the food they eat. The map below shows the world's grasslands and three birds that look similar because they have all adapted to live in similar grassland habitats. This is known as convergent evolution. The ostrich, the emu, and the rhea are probably related, but there are other examples of convergent evolution where the birds are not related at all. For example, the toucans of South America look like the hornbills of Africa and Asia, although they do not belong to the same family.

Emu
(*Dromaius novaehollandiae*)
Australia

Greater rhea
(*Rhea americana*)
South America

Ostrich
(*Struthio camelus*)
Africa

NORTH AMERICA · EUROPE · ASIA · AFRICA · SOUTH AMERICA · AUSTRALIA · ATLANTIC OCEAN · PACIFIC OCEAN · INDIAN OCEAN

POLAR AND TUNDRA
The Arctic in the north and the Antarctic in the south are among the harshest environments on Earth. Freezing temperatures, howling gales, and long, dark winters mean that few birds can live there, but seabirds nest along the coasts in summer. Surrounding the Arctic is a cold, treeless region called the tundra. In summer, birds such as waders, ducks, and geese flock there to raise their young because there are few enemies, plenty of food, and it is light all the time.

Find out more: pages 8-9, 58-59

CONIFEROUS FOREST
Coniferous trees such as pine, fir, and spruce grow in a huge forest called the taiga, which stretches across the top of North America, Europe, and Asia. The taiga is one of the largest forest areas in the world. Most coniferous trees have needle-like leaves that stay on the trees all year round. Birds feed on the tree cones and help to spread the tree seeds. Summers are usually mild, but winters are bitterly cold. Many birds fly south to warmer places in winter.

Find out more: pages 12-13, 28-29, 36-37

DECIDUOUS WOODLANDS
Deciduous, or broadleaved, woodlands grow south of the dark conifer woods. Many of the trees, such as oak and beech, lose their leaves in winter, but there is plenty of rainfall all year round and the climate is generally mild. These woodlands provide plenty of food and nesting places for birds in spring and summer.

Find out more: pages 12-13, 52-53

GRASSLANDS
Grasslands occur where the climate is too dry and the soil is too poor for most trees to survive. Fires are common in this habitat, but the grasses grow back. Grasslands provide plenty of food for seed- and insect-eating birds. Tropical grasslands, such as the African savannah, are hot all year round with long dry spells. Temperate grasslands such as the South American pampas, are cooler, with hot summers and long, cold winters.

Find out more: pages 23-24, 38-39

ISLAND EVOLUTION

Many rare and unusual birds live on islands, such as the Hawaiian Islands (shown below), the Galapagos Islands, Madagascar, and Japan. Island birds have developed in unique ways because they have been cut off from their relatives on the mainland for a long time. For example, on the Hawaiian Islands, a finch-like bird arrived some 15-20 million years ago. As there were few other birds to compete with it, this bird evolved into more than 40 different species called honeycreepers (p.11). Each species found its own type of habitat and food so it could live alongside other honeycreepers.

MOUNTAIN HABITATS

Mountains such as the Himalayas in Asia (right), the Andes in South America, the Rockies in North America, and the Alps in Europe, provide a wide range of bird habitats. On the lower slopes are warm forests, but these merge into grasslands and tundra higher up. Above a certain height – called the tree line – there are no trees because it is too cold for them to grow. Near the very top, the ground is covered in snow and ice and no birds can live there. Mountain birds have to cope with freezing temperatures, fierce winds, and thin air. Some birds move up and down the mountains with the seasons.

LIVING TOGETHER

In any one habitat, different species of bird live side by side. In a rich habitat, such as a deciduous woodland, various kinds of bird can live on a single tree by feeding and nesting at different levels and eating different types or sizes of food. Some eat insects, while others prefer seeds. In this way, the birds share out the resources of the habitat and are more likely to survive than if they compete with each other for the same things.

Near the top of the tree, tiny birds such as blue tits and wood warblers hang from the smaller twigs and pick insects off the leaves and bark.

In the middle of the tree, birds such as spotted flycatchers dart out from a perch to catch flying insects. Woodpeckers chisel into trunks and branches to find insects. They also dig out nesting holes in the trunk.

On the woodland floor, bigger birds such as the woodcock feed and nest. These birds are usually well camouflaged among the dead leaves. Wrens and other small insect-eaters hop nimbly through the dense thickets of leaves and twigs where they are hidden from enemies.

Wood warbler
(Phylloscopus sibilatrix)

Blue tit
(Parus caerulus)

Great spotted woodpecker
(Dendrocopus major)

Spotted flycatcher
(Muscicapa striata)

Woodcock
(Scopolax rusticola)

Wren
(Troglodytes troglodytes)

SCRUBLANDS

This warm, dry, dusty habitat with tough shrubs and small trees is found mainly around the shores of the Mediterranean Sea, in California, the United States, and in parts of Australia, where it is called the outback or the bush. Many birds move, or migrate, to these scrublands during the long, hot summers when there are plenty of insects and seeds to feed on. Some fly away for the cooler, wetter winter months.

Find out more: pages 30-31, 52-53

DESERTS

Deserts cover about one-fifth of the Earth's land surface. They are a difficult habitat for birds because there is little rainfall and very high daytime temperatures. Birds have to rest in the shade during the hottest times of day and either get water from their food or fly long distances to find it. Important deserts of the world include the western deserts of North America, the Sahara, Kalahari, and Namib deserts in Africa, and the Australian deserts.

Find out more: pages 15-16, 52-53

RAINFORESTS

Rainforests grow near the Equator in the Americas, Africa, Asia, and Australasia where it is hot and wet all year round. They cover less than 10 per cent of the Earth's surface, but are home to over half of all the different species of wildlife living on the Earth. Many birds live high in the tree-tops where there is more sunlight, warmth, and food. But birds live at all levels in the forest, sharing out the food and space of this rich habitat. The largest birds live on the forest floor.

Find out more: pages 20-21, 54-55

RIVERS, MARSHES, SWAMPS, AND LAKES

Watery environments are a favourite habitat for birds. Herons, ducks, geese, and swans flock there because there are plenty of fish, insects, and water plants for them to eat and reeds and riverbanks for them to nest in. Marshes and swamps are sometimes called wetlands. Trees grow in swampy areas, but there are seldom any trees on marshland. Drainage and pollution of their wetland habitats by people is a major threat to many of these birds.

Find out more: pages 16-17, 40-41

The Arctic

THE ARCTIC REGION lies right at the top of the world. It is mainly a huge ice-covered ocean, but it also includes the northern edges of North America, Europe, Asia, and Greenland. The ice-free land in the Arctic has a low, flat tundra landscape, with many lichens, mosses, grasses, and sprawling, ground-hugging bushes.

Few birds can live in the Arctic all year round because it is so cold, particularly in winter when it is also dark all day and all night. During the few light summer months, many birds migrate to the Arctic to nest and feed. At this time of year, microscopic plants and animals in the sea grow quickly with the light and warmth. They are eaten by fish, which in turn provide food for millions of gulls, auks, and terns. On the tundra lands, some of the ice melts, flowers make seeds, and insects hatch. Waders, ducks, geese, and smaller birds, hurry to eat the seeds or insects, lay their eggs, and raise their young before flying south to escape the harsh Arctic winter.

SNOWY OWL

Like a silent, white ghost, the snowy owl glides over the Arctic tundra hunting for birds and small mammals, such as lemmings and hares. It will sometimes kill as many as 10 lemmings a day. When there is plenty of food about, these powerful owls lay lots of eggs so that their chicks have a good chance of survival, but when food is scarce, they may not bother to nest at all.

Snowy owl
(*Nyctea scandiaca*)
Length: 68 cm (2 ft 3 in)

The female, shown here, is larger than the male and has more black markings.

Food is carried in a pouch or crop. This makes the throat bulge out.

Very powerful legs and talons for attacking and carrying off heavy prey.

The male's summer breeding plumage helps him to attract a female. He becomes much paler than this in winter.

LITTLE AUK

These tiny birds look like the penguins of the Antarctic because they live and feed in a similar way. Their bodies are streamlined for swimming underwater and they use their flipper-like wings to push them along. A thick layer of fat under the skin keeps them warm in the cold Arctic seas. Millions of little auks, or dovekies as they are sometimes called, raise their young on the Arctic coasts in summer. In winter, they move south, but do not often go far south of the Arctic Circle.

LAPLAND BUNTING

In the summer months, the Lapland bunting, or longspur, migrates to the Arctic tundra to nest. There are no trees in the tundra for the male to perch on while he sings to attract females or warn off rival males. Instead, he has to stand on rocks or fly up in the air to sing. The Lapland bunting often nests in small groups for protection from predators.

Lapland bunting
(*Calcarius lapponicus*)
Length: 15 cm (6 in)

Little auk
(*Alle alle*)
Length: 20 cm (8 in)

LONG-TAILED DUCK

In the Arctic summer, the yodelling courtship call of male long-tailed ducks carries long distances across the open tundra landscape. Some birdwatchers think the call sounds like bagpipes being played. Long-tailed ducks are very good at diving and can plunge as deep as 55 m (180 ft) to chase and catch fish. In areas of shallow water, they take shellfish and other small animals from the muddy bottom.

The female has dark cheek patches.

The male has long tail feathers.

Long-tailed duck
(*Clangula hyemalis*)
Length: 47 cm (1 ft 7 in)

Male and female ducks in summer plumage, which is mainly brown with white patches. In winter, it is the opposite way round – mainly white with brown patches.

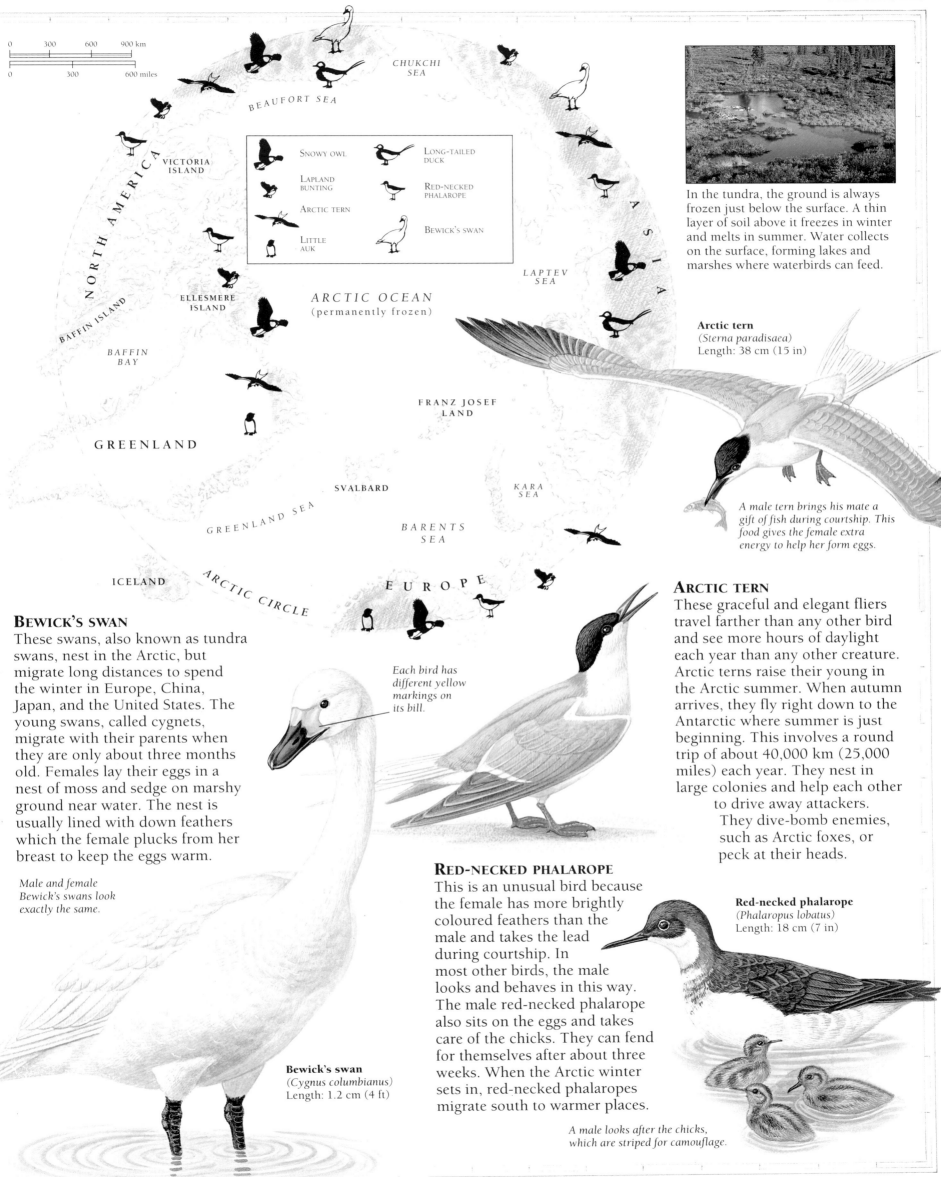

SNOWY OWL	LONG-TAILED DUCK
LAPLAND BUNTING	RED-NECKED PHALAROPE
ARCTIC TERN	
LITTLE AUK	BEWICK'S SWAN

In the tundra, the ground is always frozen just below the surface. A thin layer of soil above it freezes in winter and melts in summer. Water collects on the surface, forming lakes and marshes where waterbirds can feed.

Arctic tern
(*Sterna paradisaea*)
Length: 38 cm (15 in)

A male tern brings his mate a gift of fish during courtship. This food gives the female extra energy to help her form eggs.

ARCTIC TERN

These graceful and elegant fliers travel farther than any other bird and see more hours of daylight each year than any other creature. Arctic terns raise their young in the Arctic summer. When autumn arrives, they fly right down to the Antarctic where summer is just beginning. This involves a round trip of about 40,000 km (25,000 miles) each year. They nest in large colonies and help each other to drive away attackers. They dive-bomb enemies, such as Arctic foxes, or peck at their heads.

BEWICK'S SWAN

These swans, also known as tundra swans, nest in the Arctic, but migrate long distances to spend the winter in Europe, China, Japan, and the United States. The young swans, called cygnets, migrate with their parents when they are only about three months old. Females lay their eggs in a nest of moss and sedge on marshy ground near water. The nest is usually lined with down feathers which the female plucks from her breast to keep the eggs warm.

Male and female Bewick's swans look exactly the same.

Each bird has different yellow markings on its bill.

RED-NECKED PHALAROPE

This is an unusual bird because the female has more brightly coloured feathers than the male and takes the lead during courtship. In most other birds, the male looks and behaves in this way. The male red-necked phalarope also sits on the eggs and takes care of the chicks. They can fend for themselves after about three weeks. When the Arctic winter sets in, red-necked phalaropes migrate south to warmer places.

Red-necked phalarope
(*Phalaropus lobatus*)
Length: 18 cm (7 in)

Bewick's swan
(*Cygnus columbianus*)
Length: 1.2 cm (4 ft)

A male looks after the chicks, which are striped for camouflage.

The Americas

THE AMERICAS ARE MADE UP of two of the largest continents in the world – North America and South America. North America includes the Caribbean islands and Central America, which is the narrow strip of mountainous land that links the two continents.

South America is generally warmer than North America and contains the greatest variety of bird species on Earth. It was cut off from the other continents for millions of years and many of its birds, such as the hoatzin, the oilbird, rheas, and trumpeters are found nowhere else.

Almost half the world's bird species either breed in the tropical rainforests of South America or visit them on migration.

By contrast, North America has no unique species and its bird life is less varied. One reason for this is the large number of cities and farms in the region, but the colder climate is also important. There is less food and shelter available and many birds have to migrate to Central and South America during cold seasons. Also, the last ice ages wiped out many North American birds or drove them south.

CONTINENTS ON THE MOVE

The Earth's thin surface layer, or crust, is made up of several gigantic pieces called plates, which float on a much thicker layer of liquid rock underneath them. Powerful forces within the Earth move the plates slowly around the globe, carrying the world's great landmasses, or continents, with them. This movement is known as continental drift. The continents of North and South America have not always been in the position they are in today. Over millions of years continental drift has pulled the two continents apart and pushed them together again, altering their shape and landscape.

CLIMATE AND LANDSCAPE

The Americas stretch across the whole globe, from the Arctic in the North almost down to Antarctica in the south. All the major types of habitat in the world can be found there, including dark evergreen forests, sunny broadleaved woodlands, dry grasslands, humid rainforests, deserts, and swamps. Two huge mountain ranges – the Rockies and the Andes – stretch down the western side of the region and stop birds moving freely from east to west.

ARCTIC
OCEAN

HUDSON
BAY

NORTH
AMERICA

ROCKY MTS

GULF OF ALASKA

Mississippi

Great Lakes

Heavy storms occur in the Caribbean Sea in late summer. They can blow birds migrating from North America off course.

AMAZING BIRDS OF THE AMERICAS

Tiniest bird
The Cuban bee hummingbird is the smallest bird in the world. An adult male is only 5.7 cm (2.2 in) long.

Slowest flight
The American woodcock flies incredibly slowly for a bird at only 8 kph (5 mph).

Bee hummingbird
(Calypte helenae)

Fastest spread
In 1890, 120 starlings were introduced to New York. In only 60 years, they spread across most of North America.

Heaviest nest
The bald eagle builds the largest nest of any bird. A single nest can weigh 2,000 kg (4,400 lb), about the same as two army jeeps.

Deepest dive
The great northern diver is the deepest diving bird; it dives up to 81 m (266 ft).

Quickest runner
The greater roadrunner is the fastest-running flying bird. It runs up to 29 kph (18 mph).

Greater roadrunner
(Geococcyx californianus)

About 200 million years ago
all the continents were joined together in one landmass called Pangaea, but this was slowly beginning to break apart.

PANGAEA

About 50 million years ago
North America had separated from Europe and Asia, and South America was an island on its own. Many unique and unusual birds evolved in South America because the birds could not mix with those in other continents.

NORTH AMERICA
SOUTH AMERICA
EUROPE
ASIA
AFRICA
AUSTRALASIA
ANTARCTICA

About 3 million years ago
the continents had moved into the positions on our world map today. South America had joined on to North America. Birds could use the land bridge of Central America to move north and south between the two continents.

NORTH AMERICA
SOUTH AMERICA
EUROPE
ASIA
AFRICA
AUSTRALASIA
ANTARCTICA

ATLANTIC OCEAN

PAMPAS

Amazon

CARIBBEAN SEA

S O U T H   A M E R I C A

C E N T R A L   A M E R I C A

ANDES

ANDES

PACIFIC OCEAN

Millions of pelicans and other seabirds nest off the west coast of South America. People collect their droppings (guano) for fertilizer.

Islands
The akiapolaau is one of more than 40 species of honeycreeper that live only on the Hawaiian islands.

Rainforests
There are nearly 40 species of toucan, toucanet, and aracari living only in South American rainforests. This toco toucan is a common species.

Rivers, lakes, and swamps
Perching ducks, such as this wood duck, nest in tree holes near water. Other typical ducks of the Americas include whistling ducks, steamer ducks, teal, eider, and scoter.

Woodlands
Crows, magpies, and jays, such as this noisy blue jay, are common in the woods of North America. More than 30 species of jay live in the Americas.

Mountains
Guans, such as this shy Andean guan, live mainly in the mountain forests of Central and South America.

Grasslands
This burrowing owl lives on the grasslands and deserts of the Americas. Nearly 60 species of owl live in the Americas, including screech owls and pygmy owls.

Deserts
All the wrens in the world except for one species live in the Americas. This cactus wren prefers a desert habitat.

FACTS ABOUT THE AMERICAS

Number of birds
More than 3,100 species of bird live in South America. Colombia alone has more than 1,700 breeding species. Only about 650 species of bird live and breed in North America north of Mexico.

Largest lake
Lake Superior is the largest of the Great Lakes of North America and the largest freshwater lake in the world.

Longest mountains
The Andes are the longest mountain chain on Earth, stretching for more than 7,250 km (4,500 miles) down the west side of South America.

Long river
The Amazon in South America is the second longest river in the world, after the Nile. One-fifth of all the fresh water on Earth flows through it each day. The river pours into the Atlantic Ocean with such force that it is possible to scoop up a glass of fresh water 320 km (200 miles) out to sea.

Highest waterfall
The Angel Falls in Venezuela are the highest in the world at 979 m (3,212 ft).

Highest temperature
Death Valley in North America is one of the hottest places on Earth. Summer temperatures are often higher than 55°C (131°F).

Oldest mountains
The Appalachians are some of the oldest mountains in the world and were formed more than 250 million years ago.

TYPICAL BIRDS
Here are just a few examples of typical birds from the most important habitats of the Americas. You can find out more about them on the next few pages.

Forests and Woodlands

A HUGE EXPANSE OF evergreen forest stretches right across Canada, in a broad belt up to 800 km (500 miles) wide. It is sometimes called the boreal forest – after Boreas, the Greek god of the North Wind. The cones, buds, and needles of conifer trees, such as pines and firs, provide food for grosbeaks and juncos, but the cold weather forces most birds to fly south in winter to escape the harsh climate.

To the south of these dark forests are areas of woodland, where the climate is warmer and moister. The most common trees are broadleaved species such as oak, maple, walnut, and hickory, which lose their leaves in winter. There is a much greater variety of food and nesting places in these sunlit woods than in the dark conifer forests further north. The carpet of decaying leaves on the woodland floor is inhabited by tiny creatures that birds can eat.

BALD EAGLE

The national bird of the United States, the bald eagle, has a spectacular courtship display. A male and a female bird lock talons together and somersault through the air. The pair make a gigantic nest called an eyrie. It is built in a tree or on a rocky cliff and made of sticks, weeds, and soil. The birds use the nest year after year and keep adding to it.

The white feathers on its head grow only after the bird is four years old.

Fish such as salmon are a common source of food for the eagle.

Bald eagle
(Haliaeetus leucocephalus)
Length: 81 cm (2 ft 8 in)
Wingspan: up to 2.2 m (7 ft 2 in)

Maple trees in broadleaved woodlands turn spectacular shades of red and gold before losing their leaves for the winter.

YELLOW-BELLIED SAPSUCKER

The yellow-bellied sapsucker drills neat rows of holes in trees, such as birches, and waits for the sap to ooze out and run down the trunk. Then it laps up the sugary sap with its brush-like tongue. Insects sometimes get trapped in the sticky liquid and the sapsucker eats these as well. In winter, the yellow-bellied sapsucker migrates south to the warmer climates of Central America and the Caribbean islands.

Yellow-bellied sapsucker
(Sphyrapicus varius)
Length: 21 cm (8 in)

The sapsucker presses its tail against the tree trunk to prop itself up.

If a covey is disturbed, the birds fly off in different directions to confuse enemies and give the birds time to escape.

Northern bobwhite
(Colinus virginianus)
Length: 25 cm (10 in)

NORTHERN BOBWHITE

Outside the breeding season, bobwhites gather in groups of between 15 and 30 birds, called coveys. Each covey defends its own special area from other coveys. At night, a covey huddles on the ground in a circle. The birds sit with their heads pointing outwards to face danger and their bodies touching to keep warm.

| 0 | 250 | 500 | 750 km |

| 0 | 250 | 500 miles |

ARCTIC OCEAN

GULF OF ALASKA

Great Bear Lake

Great Slave Lake

NORTH AMERICA

PACIFIC OCEAN

ROCKY MTS

Rio Grande

YELLOW-BELLIED SAPSUCKER   NORTHERN CARDINAL

WHIP-POOR-WILL   BALD EAGLE

RUFFED GROUSE

NORTHERN BOBWHITE   AMERICAN ROBIN

OWLS – THE NIGHT HUNTERS

Owls are one of the most characteristic birds of woodland areas. They have short, rounded wings so they can fly easily between the trees. They have large eyes and can turn their heads right round to see behind them. Most owls are night hunters, using their sharp hearing and eyesight to catch food in the dark. Owls collect sounds in their round faces, which act like radar dishes and funnel the sounds to their ear openings. The openings lie under feathered flaps of skin on the sides of their faces.

Owls have powerful legs with needle-sharp, curved talons for gripping prey.

Flight feathers have a soft fringe to break up the flow of air and muffle the sound of the wings. Owls make very little noise as they fly.

The owl's outer toe can point either forwards or backwards for extra grip.

The woodland owl swoops silently down from a perch, swinging its feet forwards at the last minute to grab its prey. It swallows prey, such as mice and voles, whole, head first. It cannot digest bones, fur, or feathers, so it coughs these up in the form of pellets.

NORTHERN CARDINAL

Northern cardinals have a rich variety of songs and males and females may sing in turn as if replying to each other. Unlike other birds that live in territories just for the breeding season, they sing all year round to keep other birds away. The cardinal is named after the bright red robes worn by Roman Catholic cardinals.

Male

Female

The male cardinal is more colourful than the female.

Northern cardinal
(*Cardinalis cardinalis*)
Length: 22 cm (9 in)

Ruffed grouse
(*Bonasa umbellus*)
Length: 43 cm (17 in)

RUFFED GROUSE

In spring, the male ruffed grouse often sits on a log and makes a drumming sound by beating his wings to and fro. The sound gets faster and faster, carrying a long way through the forest and helping to attract a female. She nests among aspen trees, feeding on the tree catkins while she sits on her eggs to keep them warm. In winter, ruffed grouse grow comb-like bristles on their toes that act as snowshoes.

The male beats his wings to attract a mate.

During his display, the male spreads out his tail like a fan.

Mottled feathers ensure the whip-poor-will is well camouflaged among dead leaves.

Whip-poor-will
(*Caprimulgus vociferus*)
Length: 25 cm (10 in)

WHIP-POOR-WILL

During the day, the whip-poor-will sleeps on the forest floor. Its mottled colours match the dead leaves so it is hard to see. At night, it flies near to the ground with its mouth open, scooping up flying insects. The bird is so named because of its call which sounds like "whip-poor-will". It may repeat the call a hundred times or more without stopping.

Keen eyesight for finding worms.

American robin
(*Turdus migratorius*)
Length: 25 cm (10 in)

HUDSON BAY

St. Lawrence

ATLANTIC OCEAN

Great Lakes

APPALACHIAN MTS.

Mississippi

AMERICAN ROBIN

This robin originally nested in open woodlands but has adapted well to suburban gardens. It often builds a nest on a house porch or in a nearby tree. It eats insects and worms, but also likes fruit, especially in winter. It sometimes spends the winter in northern conifer forests, gathering in large roosts of thousands of birds.

13

Western Mountains

THE WESTERN MOUNTAIN RANGES, such as the Rockies, the Cascade Range, and the Sierra Nevada, provide a variety of habitats for birds, concentrated in a small space. The warm, wet weather on the lower mountain slopes encourages the growth of dense forests. These forests shelter and feed many birds, from woodpeckers and nutcrackers to jays and chickadees. Higher up the mountains, it is cooler and drier and the forests give way to grassy meadows and bare, rocky ground on the frozen peaks. Here, eagles and other birds of prey soar aloft on rising air currents, which sweep over the mountains. A few unusual birds, such as ptarmigans, survive on the higher slopes; their downy feathers keep them warm.

BLACK-BILLED MAGPIE

The black-billed magpie is an adaptable bird that eats a range of foods, especially insects and small rodents. It often perches on the backs of cattle and sheep to pick off the ticks and maggots living on their skin. It builds a large, strong nest of twigs, mud, and plant material, lined with fine grass and hair. A dome of sticks, often thorny ones, protects the top of the nest from enemies.

WHITE-TAILED PTARMIGAN

In winter, this ptarmigan grows white feathers which camouflage it against the snowy landscape. It often crouches low down in the snow to keep out of the fierce, cold mountain winds and avoid enemies. It tends to run away from danger instead of flying. In the summer breeding season, it grows mottled brown feathers. These are very useful to the female, as they hide her while she is sitting on her eggs.

Golden eagle
(Aquila chrysaetos)
Length: up to 1 m (3 ft 3 in)
Wingspan: up to 2 m (6 ft 6 in)

Powerful, hooked bill for tearing flesh from prey.

Strong talons for gripping prey, such as this rabbit, and flying with it.

GOLDEN EAGLE

To hunt for food, the golden eagle soars high up in the sky on its powerful wings. When its sharp eyes spot a small mammal, it dives quickly down to seize its prey and crush it in its hooked talons. The golden eagle will attack animals as big as deer, especially in winter when other food is scarce. It nests on rocky crags or in tall trees and the nest of sticks can be enormous.

Black-billed magpie
(Pica pica)
Length: 50 cm (20 in)

Tail is longer than the body.

Vast areas of coniferous forest at the base of the Rockies shelter birds from harsh weather.

White-tailed ptarmigan
(Lagopus leucurus)
Length: 32 cm (12 in)

Mountain chickadee
(Parus gambeli)
Length: 15 cm (6 in)

MOUNTAIN CHICKADEE

In spring and summer, the mountain chickadee nests in the mountain forests, but it moves down to warmer valleys in the cold winter months. There it joins flocks of other small birds, such as wood warblers and vireos, that roam the valley forests searching for food. If chickadees kept to their own territories in winter, they would not find enough food to eat.

The chickadee feeds on insects and seeds in conifers, such as this douglas fir.

Feathers for keeping feet warm. Scales on toes act as snowshoes to stop the bird sinking into snow.

Deserts

The hot, dry deserts of the southwestern United States are home to a surprising variety of birds. To cope with the heat, birds rest in the shade of rocks or down burrows dug by desert mammals. There is little water to drink – the Sonoran Desert receives less than 20 cm (8 in) of rain a year and the Great Basin deserts only 4 cm (1.5 in) a year. Birds are forced to get most of the water they need from their food, such as seeds, other animals, and water-filled cacti. The spiny branches of cacti help to protect the nests of many birds and some, such as the saguaro, are so big that birds can nest inside them. It is much cooler inside the cactus, out of the heat of the sun. In the Great Basin Desert, the many sagebrush bushes are rich in energy-giving fats for birds to eat.

A gila woodpecker perches on a giant desert cactus to feed insects to its young nesting inside.

ROCKY MTS

PACIFIC OCEAN

GREAT BASIN

DEATH VALLEY

MOJAVE DESERT

SONORAN DESERT

ROCKY MTS

GREAT PLAINS

Arkansas

Red River

Rio Grande

SIERRA MADRE OCCIDENTAL

GULF OF CALIFORNIA

GULF OF MEXICO

GOLDEN EAGLE		ELF OWL	
BLACK-BILLED MAGPIE		CACTUS WREN	
MOUNTAIN CHICKADEE		WHITE-TAILED PTARMIGAN	
		GREATER ROADRUNNER	

CACTUS WREN

This is the largest North American wren. Like other wrens, it builds several nests – some to sleep in, some to shelter in, and a few for the eggs and young. Each nest is a domed shape with a tunnel-like entrance and is built on a prickly cholla cactus or a spiny yucca or mesquite tree. The wren doesn't seem to mind the sharp spines but enemies find it hard to reach the nest.

0   200   400   600 km

0   200   400 miles

Cactus wren
(*Campylorhynchus brunneicapillus*)
Length: 21 cm (8 in)

GREATER ROADRUNNER

The roadrunner is really a type of cuckoo that lives on the ground. Even though it is often seen on roads, it is a shy bird that runs rapidly away from danger. It also chases anything that moves. On its long, powerful legs, it can sprint at up to 24 kph (15 mph), fluttering its stubby wings for extra speed. Its long tail acts as a brake to help the bird stop or change direction.

Elf owl
(*Microthene whitneyi*)
Length: 15 cm (6 in)

ELF OWL

This is the smallest owl in the world – it is no bigger than an adult's hand. It feeds mainly at night, catching insects in its feet. It will also eat scorpions, taking out the sting or crushing it before starting to eat. To escape the heat of the sun, it roosts by day in holes in giant cacti dug by other birds. If captured, the elf owl pretends to be dead until it thinks the danger has passed.

The roadrunner has a very varied diet that includes lizards, mice, insects, and even small rattlesnakes.

Greater roadrunner
(*Geococcyx californianus*)
Length: 60 cm (2 ft)

Rivers, Lakes, and Swamps

NORTH AMERICA'S RIVERS, lakes, and swamps are a rich environment for birds because of the variety of food and nesting places they provide. Many marshes were once protected so people could hunt the ducks and geese, but they are now nature reserves. In the southeast are swamps dominated by bald cypress trees draped with vines, Spanish moss, and orchids. These include the Florida Everglades and the "bayous" of the Mississippi delta. There are an amazing number of ponds and lakes in North America. Some formed where ice sheets dug hollows in the land. Others formed as a result of movements of the Earth's crust. Many rivers, lakes, and swamps are threatened by the pollution caused by farms and factories.

Head and neck are stretched out in flight.

Jet black wing-tips.

WHOOPING CRANE
The whooping crane is one of the world's most endangered birds. It almost died out in the 1940s but its numbers are now increasing due to conservation. The whooping crane nests in northwestern Canada but migrates south to the warmer weather of Texas in winter. Its name comes from its loud, trumpeting call.

Whooping crane
(Grus americana)
Length: 1.3 m (4 ft 3 in)

COMMON LOON
The common loon, or great northern diver, as it is sometimes known, can plunge up to 81 m (266 ft) below the waters of lakes and rivers. Its feet are set well back on its body to push it through the water when it dives but it finds it hard to walk on dry land. It sometimes produces a mournful, yodelling call or wails and laughs wildly. These eerie calls can often be heard at night.

Common loon
(Gavia immer)
Length: 90 cm
(2 ft 11 in)

Winter

Summer

ROSEATE SPOONBILL	ANHINGA
BELTED KINGFISHER	COMMON LOON
WHOOPING CRANE	SNAIL KITE
GREEN-BACKED HERON	

Belted kingfisher
(Megaceryle alcyon)
Length: 33 cm (13 in)

The female is a chestnut colour on her chest and flanks.

In winter the loon's plumage is much paler and duller than it is in summer.

Great Bear Lake

Great Slave Lake

ROCKY MTS

N O R T H
A M E R I C A

Stout, sharp bill for spearing fish.

BELTED KINGFISHER
This kingfisher usually hovers over the water, then plunges in to grab a fish in its strong beak. It also swoops close to the water's surface and dips down to catch a meal. It has a loud, rattling call, often made as it flies. The female lays her eggs at the end of a long tunnel in a steep bank near the water.

Lakes surrounded by coniferous forest, like this one on the north-west coast of Canada, are home to birds such as loons and cranes.

Great Lakes

St. Lawrence

APPALACHIAN MTS

PACIFIC OCEAN

Colorado

Rio Grande

SIERRA MADRE

Red

Mississippi

GULF OF MEXICO

Large broad wings help the bird to soar.

The Everglades (see map on facing page.)

0   250   500   750 km

0   250   500 miles

The Everglades

The tropical swamps of the Everglades National Park in southern Florida are home to a unique variety of birds. Many migrating birds stop and rest here too. The whole area is only just above sea level and consists of a huge swamp covered with sedges, grasses, and rushes. Deeper channels of open water run through it. These contain islands of trees called hummocks. Along the coast, belts of mangrove trees trap mud and silt with their roots and build up new land. The birds feed on the variety of insects and fish that live in this warm, humid environment.

EVERGLADES

GULF OF MEXICO

FLORIDA BAY

ATLANTIC OCEAN

FLORIDA KEYS

0   10   20   30 km

0   10   20 miles

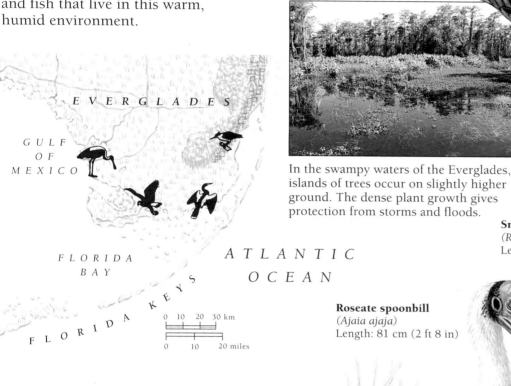

In the swampy waters of the Everglades, islands of trees occur on slightly higher ground. The dense plant growth gives protection from storms and floods.

SNAIL KITE

This unusual kite feeds only on water snails of the group known as apple snails, or *Pomacea*. It flaps slowly over the swamps on its large, wide wings. When it spots a snail, it swoops down, grabs the snail in one foot, and carries it to a perch. Then it uses its thin, hooked bill to pull out the body of the snail without breaking the shell. Snail kites in the Everglades were once near to extinction but they are now a protected species.

Long, hooked upper bill.

Snail kite
(*Rostrhamus sociabilis*)
Length: 46 cm (18 in)

Male has red legs; female and young have orange legs.

Roseate spoonbill
(*Ajaia ajaja*)
Length: 81 cm (2 ft 8 in)

Broad tip to the long bill is like a spoon.

Ear opening on the side of the head.

ROSEATE SPOONBILL

Nesting colonies of spoonbills are a spectacular sight in the Everglades. They have elaborate courtship displays, including clapping bills and giving each other twigs. To catch food, the spoonbill sweeps its sensitive bill from side to side through the water. When it feels food, such as fish, it snaps its bill quickly shut. Spoonbills were once hunted for their feathers, which were used to decorate hats. They are now protected and their numbers have grown.

GREEN-BACKED HERON

The shy green-backed heron feeds mainly at night and hides among waterside plants by day. But it has adapted well to living in urban areas near people. It grabs fish and small animals in its long, strong bill and will sometimes dive underwater to chase its prey.

The female has a tawny brown neck and breast.

Large, broad wings are spread out to dry in the sun.

ANHINGA

The anhinga often swims on the surface with just its head and neck showing, so it looks like a snake. For this reason it is sometimes called a snakebird. It dives deep under the water to catch fish, spearing them with its dagger-like bill. The jagged edges of its bill help the anhinga to keep a firm hold on its prey until it can flip it up into the air and swallow it whole.

Crest is raised when the bird is excited.

The green-backed heron often crouches silent and still at the edge of water to spot its prey.

Green-backed heron
(*Butorides striatus*)
Length: 48 cm
(1 ft 9 in)

Anhinga
(*Anhinga anhinga*)
Length: 91 cm (3 ft)

Central America and the Caribbean

THE RICH BIRD LIFE of Central America is partly due to the variety of landscapes in the region, which vary from dry grassland on the west coast to alpine meadows on the mountains in the middle, and lush rainforest and swamps on the eastern coasts. Central America forms a narrow bridge linking North and South America, so birds from both continents mix there. Many North American birds migrate to the warmer climate of Central America for the winter.

The Caribbean islands are the tips of mountains buried in very deep water. The birds here are either strong fliers that were able to reach the islands or birds blown there accidentally by strong winds. Several unique species have developed on the islands: the tody family, for example, is found nowhere else in the world.

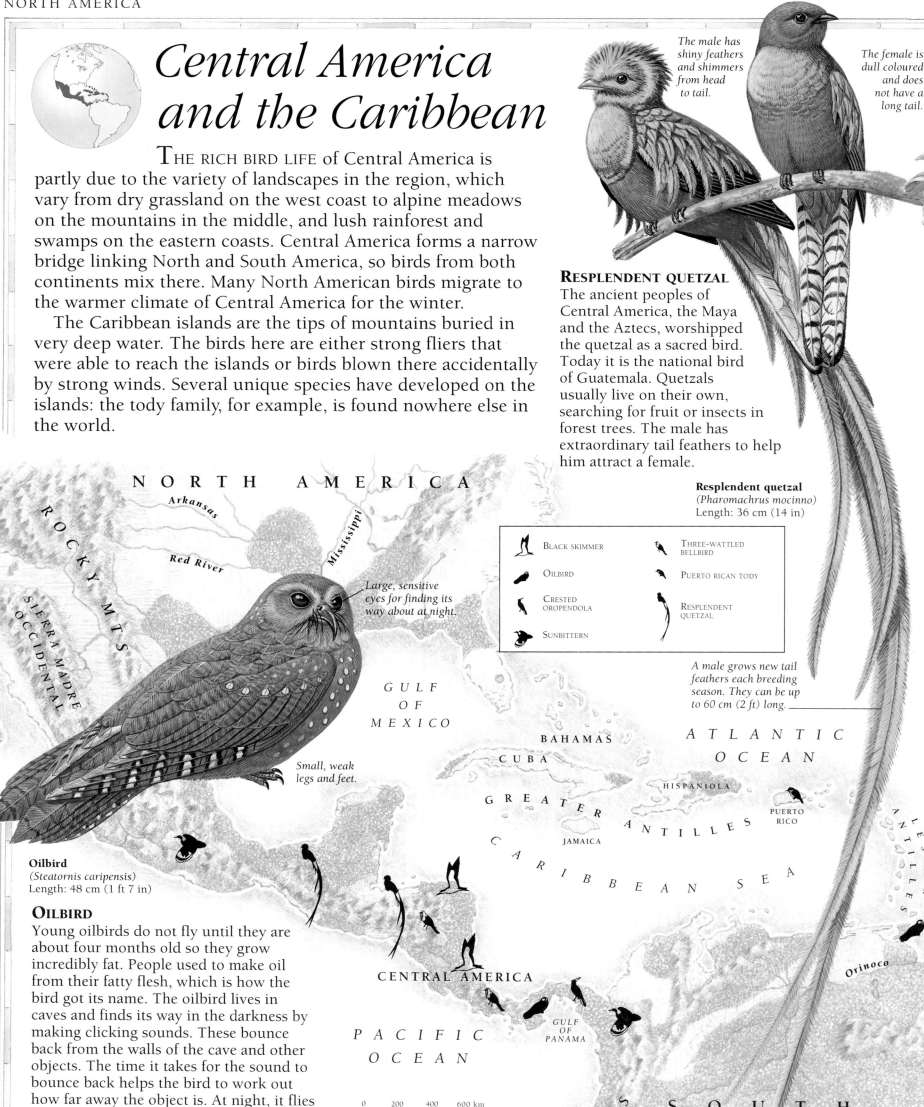

The male has shiny feathers and shimmers from head to tail.

The female is dull coloured and does not have a long tail.

RESPLENDENT QUETZAL

The ancient peoples of Central America, the Maya and the Aztecs, worshipped the quetzal as a sacred bird. Today it is the national bird of Guatemala. Quetzals usually live on their own, searching for fruit or insects in forest trees. The male has extraordinary tail feathers to help him attract a female.

Resplendent quetzal
(*Pharomachrus mocinno*)
Length: 36 cm (14 in)

A male grows new tail feathers each breeding season. They can be up to 60 cm (2 ft) long.

NORTH AMERICA

Arkansas

Red River

Mississippi

ROCKY MTS

SIERRA MADRE OCCIDENTAL

Large, sensitive eyes for finding its way about at night.

GULF OF MEXICO

Small, weak legs and feet.

	BLACK SKIMMER		THREE-WATTLED BELLBIRD
	OILBIRD		PUERTO RICAN TODY
	CRESTED OROPENDOLA		RESPLENDENT QUETZAL
	SUNBITTERN		

BAHAMAS

CUBA

ATLANTIC OCEAN

HISPANIOLA

GREATER ANTILLES

PUERTO RICO

JAMAICA

LESSER ANTILLES

CARIBBEAN SEA

Oilbird
(*Steatornis caripensis*)
Length: 48 cm (1 ft 7 in)

OILBIRD

Young oilbirds do not fly until they are about four months old so they grow incredibly fat. People used to make oil from their fatty flesh, which is how the bird got its name. The oilbird lives in caves and finds its way in the darkness by making clicking sounds. These bounce back from the walls of the cave and other objects. The time it takes for the sound to bounce back helps the bird to work out how far away the object is. At night, it flies out of the cave to feed on oily fruits. Its good sense of smell and excellent eyesight help it to find food.

CENTRAL AMERICA

PACIFIC OCEAN

GULF OF PANAMA

Orinoco

0   200   400   600 km

0   200   400 miles

ANDES

SOUTH AMERICA

Negro

Each woven nest is over 1 m (3 ft 3 in) long and hangs from a tree branch.

CRESTED OROPENDOLA

Crested oropendolas live in groups and nest together too. They can build up to 100 nests in just one tree. This probably helps to protect the eggs and young from enemies, as the birds can warn each other of danger. The male has a spectacular courtship display to attract a female. He makes a series of loud gurgling sounds while flapping his wings and leaning forwards so far he almost falls off his perch.

Crested oropendola
(Psarocolius decumanus)
Length: 43 cm (17 in)

SUNBITTERN

During its courtship display, the sunbittern spreads its wings to show off the patches of orange and yellow colours on its feathers. These look like the colours of a sky at sunset, which is how the bird got its name. At other times, the mottled colours on the feathers camouflage the bird as it searches for food along stream banks in woodland areas. It catches fish, insects, and frogs, seizing its prey with its long, sharp bill.

Sunbittern
(Eurypyga helias)
Length: 46 cm (18 in)

Mouth opens very wide to allow the bird to swallow large fruits.

Wattles hang from top of bill and edge of mouth.

Three-wattled bellbird
(Procnias tricarunculata)
Length: 30 cm (12 in)

Jerks its head all the time while perched.

Long, straight bill for snapping up insects.

THREE-WATTLED BELLBIRD

Male bellbirds make probably the loudest noise of any bird. They advertise for a female by producing an explosive "bock" noise. This call can be heard 1 km (0.6 miles) away. The female builds the nest and looks after the young. She is a dull colour to camouflage her while she sits on the nest.

PUERTO RICAN TODY

This tody lives in woods and forests and feeds by pouncing on insects from a perch. When it flies, it makes a whirring noise with its wings. During the breeding season, the tody uses its bill to dig tiny nesting burrows in a bank, like its relative the kingfisher. There are four other species of Caribbean tody.

Puerto Rican tody
(Todus mexicanus)
Length: 10 cm (4 in)

Wings are spread out during courtship displays.

Black skimmer
(Rynchops niger)
Length: 50 cm (1 ft 8 in)

BLACK SKIMMER

The black skimmer has a strange bill – the bottom part is about one-third longer than the top part. To find food, the skimmer flies over shallow water with its bill open, ploughing a furrow through the water. When its bill hits a small fish or crustacean, the skimmer snaps the top bill down like a pair of scissors to trap its prey.

Dense jungle vegetation is typical of Central America's tropical rainforests.

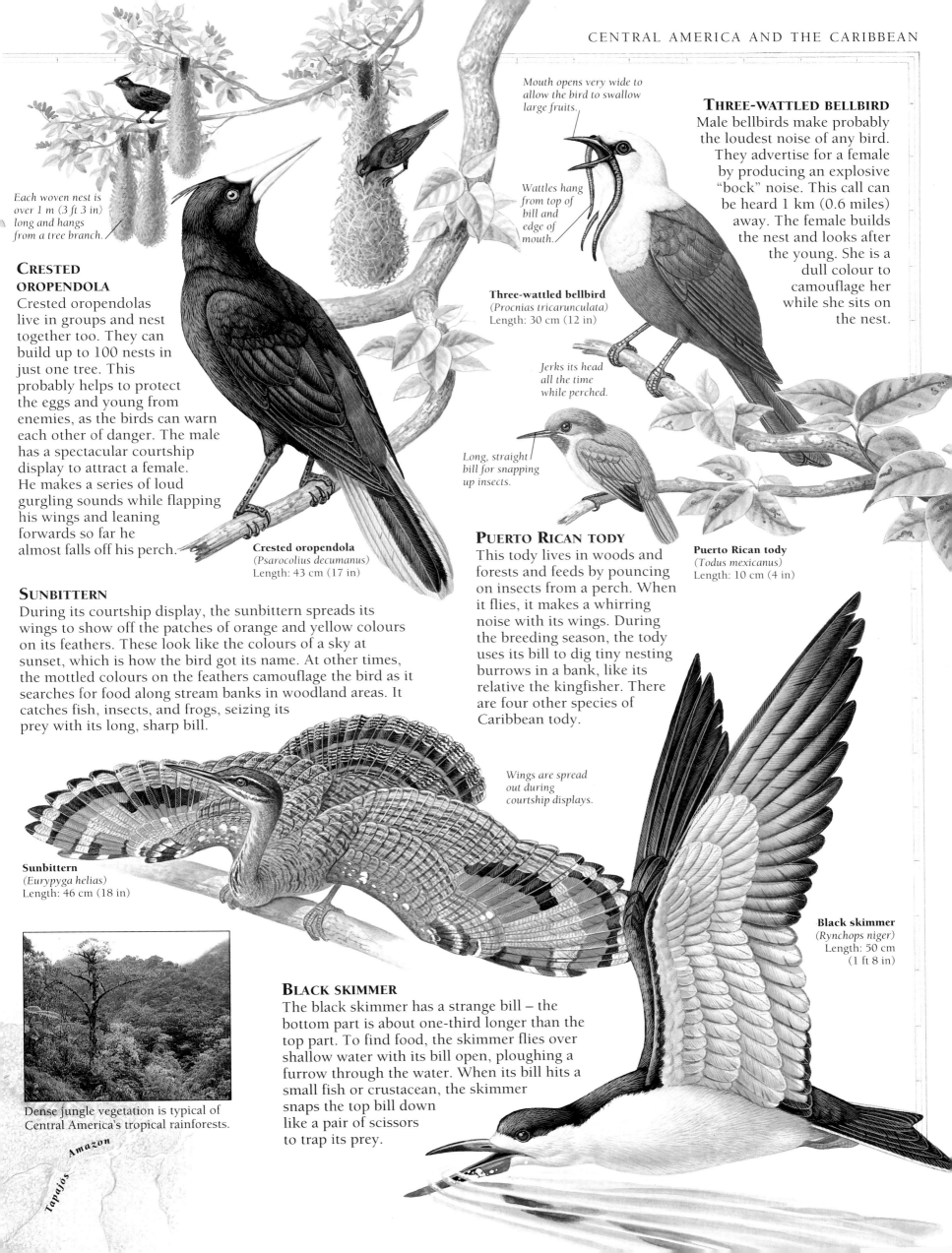

The Amazon Rainforest

THE AMAZON RAINFOREST stretches from the Andes Mountains in the west to the Atlantic Ocean in the east. One-fifth of all the kinds of birds in the world live there. This is mainly due to differences in rainfall, soils, and height of the land across the region, which provide a variety of habitats. Birds live at different layers in the trees, rather like people live in a block of flats. Each layer receives different amounts of sunlight and provides different kinds of food. Birds such as toucans live in the tree-tops, called the canopy. In the middle layers live birds such as macaws and jacamars, while down on the forest floor larger birds stalk among the fallen leaves.

CUVIER'S TOUCAN
With its long bill, Cuvier's toucan can reach out to pluck berries or seeds from trees high in the canopy. The jagged edges of its bill work like a saw to cut fruits. It also eats insects, spiders, and small birds. If its bill were as heavy as it looks, the toucan would not be able to hold up its head. In fact its bill is hollow and extremely light. The brightly coloured bill may help it to recognize others of its kind.

Cuvier's toucan
(Ramphastos cuvieri)
Length: 50 cm (1 ft 8 in)

SCARLET MACAW
At sunrise the scarlet macaw flies through the forest in search of food. It squawks noisily while flying but feeds in silence. Two of its toes point forwards and two point backwards so it can use its feet to grip well and hold food up to its mouth.

The macaw's powerful bill can crush the hardest seeds and nuts. It is also used for preening and to grip branches.

Scarlet macaw
(Ara macao)
Length: 85 cm (2 ft 9 in)

Short legs help the macaw to keep its balance.

COCK-OF-THE-ROCK
During courtship the male cock-of-the-rock performs amazing displays on the forest floor to attract a female. Up to 25 males display together and each has his own area. They show off by leaping into the air, bobbing their heads, snapping their bills and flicking and fanning their feathers.

Cock-of-the-rock
(Rupicola rupicola)
Length: 32 cm (13 in)

Female cock-of-the-rocks are drab-coloured for camouflage and look very different from males.

During his display the male spreads his crest forwards so it almost hides his bill.

The male displays on a bare patch of forest floor called a "lek".

ATLANTIC OCEAN

Orinoco

AMAZON RAINFOREST

Negro

Amazon

Amazon

SOUTH AMERICA

ANDES

PACIFIC OCEAN

Lake Titicaca

	HARPY EAGLE		WHITE-PLUMED ANTBIRD
	WHITE-TIPPED SICKLEBILL		SCARLET MACAW
	HOATZIN		
	CUVIER'S TOUCAN		COCK-OF-THE-ROCK

0   200   400   800 km
0   250   500 miles

Rainforest birds are often brightly coloured but they are hard to see against a background of leaves and patches of sunlight.

Two toes point forwards and two point backwards to give a strong grip.

Toucans live in groups and often play games. They wrestle with their bills or toss fruit to each other, like we play "catch".

The Amazon is the world's largest tropical rainforest. It covers an area about three-quarters the size of the United States but it is being cleared at a rapid rate.

Powerful, hooked bill for tearing flesh from food.

Massive, sharp talons enable the eagle to grab and crush prey.

The harpy eagle pursues capuchin monkeys and other small animals, such as opossums and coatis, through the rainforest.

HARPY EAGLE

The huge and fearsome harpy eagle swoops through the tree-tops seeking its prey. It can fly at speeds of up to 80 kph (50 mph). Its grey, mottled colouring helps to camouflage it among the leaves so the animals it hunts do not see it coming. A pair of harpy eagles builds a nest of sticks high up in the trees.

Harpy eagle
(*Harpia harpyja*)
Length: 1.1 m (3 ft 6 in)

WHITE-TIPPED SICKLEBILL

The sicklebill is a hummingbird. Hummingbirds are named after the sound made by their wings, which flap at over 100 beats a second. The sicklebill's long curved bill helps it to reach the sweet nectar inside flowers. Its tongue forms a tube like a straw through which it can suck up nectar. Nectar is easy to digest, so it provides instant energy to power the hummingbird's whirring wings and help it to keep warm.

White-tipped sicklebill
(*Eutoxeres aquila*)
Length: 13 cm (5 in)

WHITE-PLUMED ANTBIRD

Despite its name, the white-plumed antbird does not eat ants. It follows army ants and feeds on the spiders and insects that are trying to escape them. Usually the antbird darts down to the ground or hangs from a branch to snatch up a meal. But sometimes it will hop amongst the ants, holding its tail up out of the way. Its long legs help to protect its body from the ants' stings.

Columns of army ants swarming over the forest floor.

White-plumed antbird
(*Pithys albifrons*)
Length: 11 cm (4 in)

HOATZIN

The hoatzin has weak wings and it flaps clumsily through flooded parts of the rainforest along quiet riverbanks. It uses its wings and tail to help it clamber through the trees as its feet are not very strong. Hoatzins move about and nest in groups, building untidy twig nests by the water. Young hoatzins leave the nest soon after hatching and may leap into the water to escape danger.

Hoatzin
(*Opisthocomus hoazin*)
Length: 66 cm (2 ft 2 in)

A baby hoatzin has two tiny claws on the bend of each wing to help it grip and climb.

The Andes

THE ANDES ARE THE world's longest mountain chain, running down the entire western coast of South America. The steep slopes act as a barrier to birds, so that species on the east side of the mountains differ from those on the west. Plant-life in the Andes also varies dramatically over short distances, creating a variety of habitats. These range from rainforests on the lower slopes, through drier forests and grass plains higher up, to frozen wilderness near the peaks. On the upper slopes, it is so cold that some hummingbirds go into semi-hibernation at night, slowing down all their body processes and lowering their body temperature, so they use less energy.

TORRENT DUCK

The fast-flowing rivers and streams of the Andes are home to the torrent duck. Its sharp claws and powerful legs help it to cling to slippery rocks, while its stiff tail is useful for balancing and steering in the water. It dives underwater to catch food, such as insects, but it also picks up food as it floats past on the surface. Ducklings are able to swim with their parents as soon as they hatch.

Streamlined body shape for swimming fast under the water.

Torrent duck
(Merganetta armata)
Length: 46 cm (18 in)

ANDEAN CONDOR

This huge vulture is the world's heaviest bird of prey, weighing up to 14 kg (31 lb). The Andean condor soars for long distances on outstretched wings, sometimes rising to heights of 7,000 m (23,000 ft) over the mountains. It has very keen eyesight and can spot dead animals to feed on from high up in the sky. It will also kill sick or wounded animals. Some Andean condors raid seabird colonies on the coast and take the eggs and chicks.

Bare head enables the bird to reach into a carcass without getting its feathers dirty.

The condor probably has the greatest wingspan of any land bird.

Andean condor
(Vultur gryphus)
Length: 1.1 m (3 ft 6 in)
Wingspan: up to 3 m (10 ft)

Sword-billed hummingbird
(Ensifera ensifera)
Length: 7.5 cm (3 in)
Length of bill: 10.5 cm (4 in)

Long bill for reaching pollen inside fuchsias and other trumpet-shaped flowers.

SWORD-BILLED HUMMINGBIRD

This bird's extraordinary bill enables it to reach nectar and insects deep inside trumpet-shaped flowers. The hummingbird hovers below the flowers to feed. As it does so, pollen is caught on its feathers and the bird then carries this to other flowers, so pollinating the plants (helping them to produce seeds). Over half the flowers in the Andes are pollinated by hummingbirds instead of insects.

TORRENT DUCK

ANDEAN CONDOR

SWORD-BILLED HUMMINGBIRD

RUFOUS HORNERO

COMMON CARACARA

BURROWING OWL

GREATER RHEA

CARIBBEAN SEA

SOUTH AMERICA

ANDES

Negro

Amazon

Madeira

São Francisco

Japurá

Marañón

Ucayali

Areas of dense rainforest shrouded in mist cover the lower slopes of the Andes.

0   250   500   750 km
0   250   500 miles

22

The Pampas

THE GRASSY PLAINS of the pampas lie in the southeastern corner of South America. The climate is generally dry with hot summers and cool winters. Lightning can cause fires in the dry grass, and farmers also set light to the grass to encourage new shoots to grow, so many birds nest under the ground where they are safer from fires and people. Large cattle ranches on the pampas have damaged the natural environment. Only birds that can adapt to human disturbance, such as ovenbirds, have survived. Others, have died out or decreased in number. Huge flocks of rheas are no longer common.

GREATER RHEA

The rhea is very like the African ostrich, except that it has three toes on each foot instead of two. It cannot fly, but it can sprint faster than a horse, reaching speeds of 50 kph (31 mph). In the breeding season, males fight for territory and for females. Several females lay their eggs in one male's nest and he looks after the eggs and chicks.

Greater rhea
(Rhea americana)
Length: 1.5 m (5 ft)
Height: 1.3 m (4 ft 3 in)

Rheas have three strong toes with claws on each foot for defence and for running fast.

COMMON CARACARA

These chicken-sized birds of prey are related to falcons. Caracaras build their own nests, unlike true falcons that use abandoned nests. They eat a varied diet from small mammals, birds, fish, and frogs to insects and dead meat – they often join vultures to feed on a carcass. Caracaras are rather slow and lazy birds, but they have long legs and can move quickly if in danger.

Common caracara
(Polyborus plancus)
Length: 60 cm (2 ft)

Long legs for running swiftly if necessary.

BURROWING OWL

Unlike most owls, burrowing owls are often active during the day. They live in the abandoned mud burrows of other animals and spend a lot of time perched at the entrance. If disturbed, they bob up and down and make a chattering noise. Burrowing owls can run quickly over the grasslands on their long legs to catch their food, which is usually insects and small reptiles.

Burrowing owl
(Athene cunicularia)
Length: 25 cm (10 in)

This owl nests in burrows made by viscachas and other animals, but it can also dig its own.

The vast, treeless plains of the pampas provide little shelter for birds so they nest by rocks or under the ground.

RUFOUS HORNERO

The mud nest of the rufous hornero looks rather like an old-fashioned baker's oven, so these birds are sometimes called ovenbirds. (The word *hornero* means "baker" in Spanish.) It takes the bird months to build one nest, which is about twice the size of a soccer ball, yet it starts a new one each year. The rufous hornero has long legs and strides across open ground lifting its feet high in the air. It uses its strong, sharp bill to dig up worms and insect larvae.

Rufous hornero
(Furnarius rufus)
Length: 19 cm (7 in)

The nest is made of thousands of lumps of mud, reinforced with straw and baked hard in the hot sun.

Lake Titicaca

ANDES

PACIFIC OCEAN

Paraná

Uruguay

Paraná

PAMPAS

The Galapagos Islands

THE LONELY GALAPAGOS ISLANDS, which lie in the Pacific Ocean, west of South America, are like nowhere else on Earth. The islands are the tops of huge volcanoes that rose up from the seabed millions of years ago. An extraordinary variety of birds live amongst the dry cactus scrub and jagged volcanic rocks. Many of them are found only on these islands. There are two main reasons why the bird life of the Galapagos Islands is so unique. Firstly, the islands are so far from the mainland of South America that only a few birds have managed to reach them. These were able to develop into a variety of species because there was little competition for food and nesting places. Secondly, warm waters from the Pacific and cool waters from the Antarctic both flow past the islands. This means that birds usually found in cold places, such as penguins and albatrosses, live side-by-side with tropical species, such as flamingos and frigatebirds.

ISLA MARCHENA

On this flat island, the back of a giant tortoise makes a good look-out post for a passing Galapagos hawk.

GALAPAGOS ISLANDS

ISLA SAN SALVADOR

ISLA FERNANDINA

ISLA ISABELA

Tiny wings only 25 cm (10 in) long.

PACIFIC OCEAN

Flightless cormorant
(Nannopterum harrisi)
Length: 95 cm (3 ft 1 in)

DARWIN'S FINCHES

The 13 different species of Galapagos finch look similar because they probably originated from one species. But each species has a different shaped bill to eat a different food. The British naturalist Charles Darwin's studies of these birds helped him to work out his theory of evolution. This explains how plants and animals may have changed over many generations to suit their particular habitat.

Charles Darwin
1809-1882

Warbler finch
(Certhidea olivacea)
This finch has a fine, pointed bill for catching small insects.

Tree finch
(Camarhynchus parvulus)
The tree finch has a thicker bill to cope with fruit, buds, small seeds, and insects.

Ground finch
(Geospiza magnirostris)
The large ground finch has a heavy, strong bill for crushing seeds.

Woodpecker finch
(Camarhynchus pallidus)
This is one of the few birds to make and use a tool. It uses a twig as a tool to find insect grubs under bark and tease them out.

FLIGHTLESS CORMORANT

The flightless cormorant uses its small, ragged wings to balance on land and shade its chick from the hot sun. But its wings are too weak for flying or swimming. It probably lost its powers of flight because it had no enemies to fly away from and could get all its food close to the shore. Now it is the only cormorant alive that cannot fly. This made it easy for people to hunt and it became rare. Today it is a protected species.

Nests on rocks close to the sea.

GALAPAGOS PENGUIN

This rare penguin is able to live so near the Equator because of the cool waters of the Humboldt Current, which flow past the Galapagos Islands. It feeds on fish and nests in small groups, laying its eggs in nests of stones, in caves, or holes. Like all penguins, this one is well adapted for fast swimming underwater. It has wings like flippers, webbed feet, and a streamlined body shape, yet it is clumsy on land. It hops shakily from one rock to another, holding out its little flippers for balance. When it reaches the water, it jumps in feet first.

Strong flippers help the penguin "fly" under water.

Galapagos penguin
(Spheniscus mendiculus)
Length: 51 cm (1 ft 8 in)

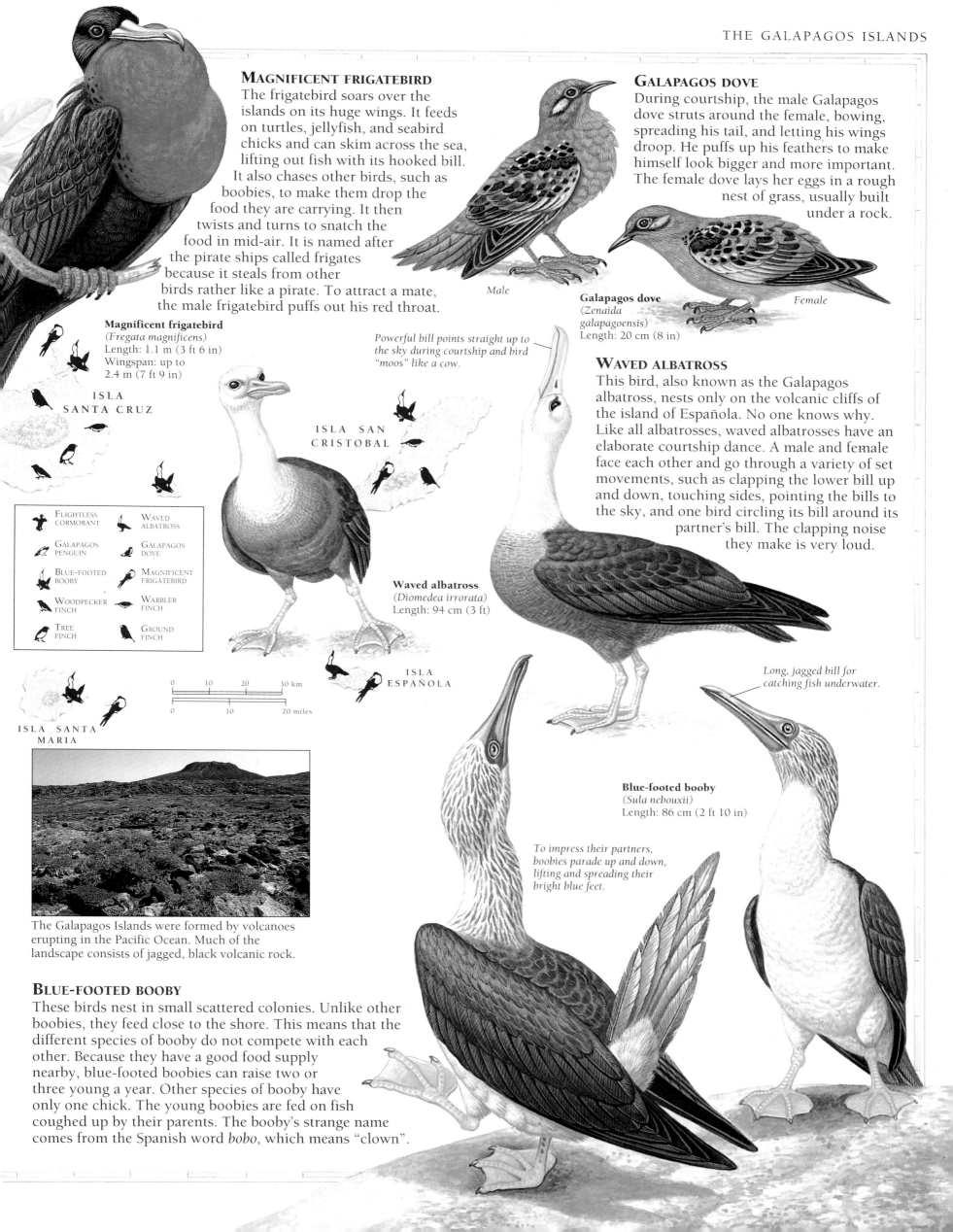

MAGNIFICENT FRIGATEBIRD

The frigatebird soars over the islands on its huge wings. It feeds on turtles, jellyfish, and seabird chicks and can skim across the sea, lifting out fish with its hooked bill. It also chases other birds, such as boobies, to make them drop the food they are carrying. It then twists and turns to snatch the food in mid-air. It is named after the pirate ships called frigates because it steals from other birds rather like a pirate. To attract a mate, the male frigatebird puffs out his red throat.

Magnificent frigatebird
(*Fregata magnificens*)
Length: 1.1 m (3 ft 6 in)
Wingspan: up to
2.4 m (7 ft 9 in)

ISLA
SANTA CRUZ

GALAPAGOS DOVE

During courtship, the male Galapagos dove struts around the female, bowing, spreading his tail, and letting his wings droop. He puffs up his feathers to make himself look bigger and more important. The female dove lays her eggs in a rough nest of grass, usually built under a rock.

Male

Galapagos dove
(*Zenaida galapagoensis*)
Length: 20 cm (8 in)

Female

Powerful bill points straight up to the sky during courtship and bird "moos" like a cow.

ISLA SAN
CRISTOBAL

WAVED ALBATROSS

This bird, also known as the Galapagos albatross, nests only on the volcanic cliffs of the island of Española. No one knows why. Like all albatrosses, waved albatrosses have an elaborate courtship dance. A male and female face each other and go through a variety of set movements, such as clapping the lower bill up and down, touching sides, pointing the bills to the sky, and one bird circling its bill around its partner's bill. The clapping noise they make is very loud.

FLIGHTLESS CORMORANT	WAVED ALBATROSS
GALAPAGOS PENGUIN	GALAPAGOS DOVE
BLUE-FOOTED BOOBY	MAGNIFICENT FRIGATEBIRD
WOODPECKER FINCH	WARBLER FINCH
TREE FINCH	GROUND FINCH

Waved albatross
(*Diomedea irrorata*)
Length: 94 cm (3 ft)

ISLA
ESPAÑOLA

ISLA SANTA
MARIA

0   10   20   30 km
0   10   20 miles

Long, jagged bill for catching fish underwater.

Blue-footed booby
(*Sula nebouxii*)
Length: 86 cm (2 ft 10 in)

To impress their partners, boobies parade up and down, lifting and spreading their bright blue feet.

The Galapagos Islands were formed by volcanoes erupting in the Pacific Ocean. Much of the landscape consists of jagged, black volcanic rock.

BLUE-FOOTED BOOBY

These birds nest in small scattered colonies. Unlike other boobies, they feed close to the shore. This means that the different species of booby do not compete with each other. Because they have a good food supply nearby, blue-footed boobies can raise two or three young a year. Other species of booby have only one chick. The young boobies are fed on fish coughed up by their parents. The booby's strange name comes from the Spanish word *bobo*, which means "clown".

Europe

THE SMALL CONTINENT of Europe has been covered by ice at least four times in the past million years. The climate in northern Europe is still very cold and many birds from this region are forced to migrate south for the winter.

Europe does not have a huge variety of bird species, partly due to the cold weather in the north, but also because of the large numbers of people that live there – many more than in North America. People have cleared away the forests, polluted the land and water, and hunted the birds. Birds that cannot live in cities, parks, or gardens have been driven to remote areas such as mountains, moorlands, and marshes. Many coastal habitats in Europe are, however, very rich in bird life. Estuaries provide vital feeding and resting areas for waterbirds and waders migrating south from the Arctic. Sea cliffs are home to nesting colonies of seabirds such as gannets, guillemots, puffins, and razorbills.

EUROPE UNDER ICE

This map shows the extent of the ice sheet 11,000 years ago – at the end of Europe's last ice age.

At various times in the Earth's history, there have been cold spells called ice ages, which have lasted for thousands of years. During an ice age, ice sheets and glaciers spread across the Earth's surface. Over the past 900,000 years, there have been about 10 major ice ages. At the height of the last ice age, about 18,000 years ago, great ice sheets spread out from the North Pole, covering much of Europe. Some birds died out, while others moved south to warmer places. About 11,000 years ago, the climate became warmer again, the ice receded and some of the birds returned north.

CLIMATE AND LANDSCAPE

The climate of Europe ranges from the cold, rainy, and snowy northern lands, such as the British Isles and Scandinavia, to the hot, dry Mediterranean lands of the south, such as Italy and Greece. In the middle are warm, wet areas with a mild climate. A warm ocean current called the Gulf Stream flows from the Caribbean past the western shores of Europe, making the winter climate on the west coast less severe. Europe's landscape includes long mountain chains, such as the Alps and the Pyrenees, which stop birds moving freely from north to south.

AMAZING BIRDS OF EUROPE

Goldcrest
(Regulus regulus)

Smallest bird
The tiny goldcrest is the smallest European bird 9 cm (3.5 in).

Fastest bird
The peregrine falcon is the fastest bird in the world. It reaches speeds of up to 180 kph (112 mph) when swooping down to chase its prey.

Strongest bill
The hawfinch has the most powerful bill and jaw muscles of any bird. It can easily crack cherry stones.

Varied eggs
The guillemot has a greater variety of colours and patterns on its eggs than any other bird. This means parents can recognize their own eggs on the crowded cliff ledges where they nest.

Largest clutch
The female grey partridge lays the most eggs at one time of any bird – as many as 15-19 eggs in one clutch. She lays so many because a large proportion of the chicks do not survive.

Marvellous mimic
The marsh warbler is the world champion bird mimic. It can copy the songs of about 76 other bird species.

Greatest stamina
The common swift spends more time in the air than any other land bird. It sleeps, eats, and drinks on the wing for up to three years at heights of up to 2,000 m (6,500 ft).

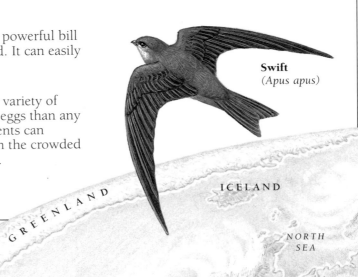

Swift
(Apus apus)

GREENLAND
ICELAND
ATLANTIC OCEAN
NORTH SEA
BRITISH ISLES
Rhine
Loire
Danube
ALPS
CORSICA
PYRENEES
Douro
SARDINIA
Guadalquivir
MEDITERRANEAN SEA
ATLAS MTS
NORTH AFRICA

Many people live and farm in the sunny Mediterranean region, growing crops such as these olives. This means there are fewer places for birds to live.

FACTS ABOUT EUROPE

Number of birds
More than 600 species of bird have been spotted in Europe. Of these, about 430 birds regularly occur there.

Longest glacier
The longest glacier in the Alps is called the Aletsch and is more than 24 km (15 miles) long.

High population
Europe occupies only about 7 per cent of the world's land area, yet 14 per cent of the world's population – a total of about 690 million people – live there.

Longest coastline
Europe has a longer coastline in proportion to its size than any other continent. Norway's coastline is indented with steep valleys called fjords (above) that were cut into the cliffs by thick glaciers during the last ice age.

Main mountains
Mont Blanc is 4,807 m (15,770 ft) tall and is western Europe's highest mountain. It forms part of the Alps mountain range, which stretches for 1,100 km (660 miles).

Volcanic eruptions
The only active volcano on mainland Europe is Vesuvius, in Italy. It began erupting 10,000 years ago and buried the towns of Pompeii and Stabiae in AD 79.

Longest rivers
The longest rivers in Europe are: the Volga – 3,531 km (2,194 miles); the Danube – 2,858 km (1,776 miles); and the Dnieper – 2,285 km (1,420 miles).

Largest sea
Europe's Mediterranean Sea is the largest sea in the world.

TYPICAL BIRDS

Here are a few examples of typical birds from the most important habitats of Europe. These range from dark conifer forests in the north, to more open broadleaved woodlands further south, and dry scrubland around the shores of the Mediterranean. Rivers, lakes, marshes, and coasts are also major European bird habitats. (You can find out more on the next few pages.)

Moorland
Birds such as this merlin nest on European moors in summer. In winter, they move to marshlands and shores where there is more food available.

Mountains
Mountains provide refuges from towns and farms for birds such as this chough, as well as golden eagles, and vultures.

Coasts
Seabirds such as this puffin, along with guillemots, gulls, gannets, and terns, nest in densely packed colonies on cliffs, beaches, and islands around the coasts of Europe in spring and summer.

Mediterranean scrub
The rich variety of insects in the Mediterranean scrublands in summer attract insect-eating birds, such as this hoopoe, along with rollers, shrikes, and honey buzzards. Many migrate south to Africa for the winter.

Towns and cities
Birds such as this pigeon, as well as starlings, sparrows, and kestrels, have made themselves at home in urban habitats. Pigeons nest on the window ledges of tall buildings as if they were cliffs by the coast.

Estuaries and shores
In winter, waders such as this redshank, along with godwits, dunlin, and curlews, gather in flocks on estuaries and shores to feed on creatures in the mud and sand.

Forests and woodlands
Warblers such as this wood warbler, along with thrushes, jays, woodpeckers, owls, and tits, are common in the remaining areas of European forests and woodlands.

EUROPE

CARPATHIAN MTS

Dnieper
Don

URAL MTS

ASIA

Danube

BLACK SEA

CAUCASUS MTS

Volga

CASPIAN SEA

ARAL SEA

CYPRUS

Tigris

Euphrates

MEDITERRANEAN SEA

Forests and Woodlands

FROM THE EVERGREEN forests of the north to the broadleaved woodland areas further south, European forests provide a rich habitat for birds. Tree trunks and branches are safe nesting places and tree leaves, nuts, and berries are good to eat. Insects and small creatures living on the trees and woodland floor are also useful food for birds. The northern forests are generally darker and colder than those further south, which have a greater variety of food and nesting places. Unfortunately, many of Europe's forests are now threatened by pollution and people clearing the land for houses or farms.

European forest and woodland birds have to arrange their lives around the seasons. In spring and summer, they nest and rear their young; in autumn, they eat as much as possible to build up stores of fat in their bodies; and in winter, they may fly south to warmer places or roam widely through the forest in search of food.

JAY

The harsh, screeching call of the jay can often be heard in broadleaved woodlands, especially in the spring, when birds chase each other noisily through the trees as part of their courtship display. Jays feed on acorns, which they often carry for long distances, and then bury to eat during the cold winter months. Acorns that are not eaten grow into new oak trees, helping the woodlands to spread. Jays also eat other nuts, berries, worms, spiders, and the eggs and young of other birds.

Crest is often raised, making the bird's head look a square shape.

Jay
(Garrulus glandarius)
Length: 33 cm (13 in)

NORTHERN SPARROWHAWK

The agile, fast-flying sparrowhawk makes swift, surprise attacks on blue tits and other small birds. They have little chance of escaping its needle-sharp talons. Before eating its prey, the sparrowhawk plucks off the bird's feathers. The female tears up food that the male has caught to feed to the young.

The female is larger than the male and has grey bars underneath.

Blue tits

Short, rounded wings allow the bird to twist and turn through trees.

Northern sparrowhawk
(Accipiter nisus)
Length: up to 38 cm (15 in)

Crossbills nest and feed high in the tree-tops of coniferous forests. They pull seeds from pine cones and rarely venture down to the forest floor.

ATLANTIC OCEAN

NORTH SEA

BRITISH ISLES

ENGLISH CHANNEL

EUROPE

BALTIC SEA

Elbe

Oder

Vistula

Rhine

Loire

Rhône

ALPS

CARPATHIAN MTS

MEDITERRANEAN SEA

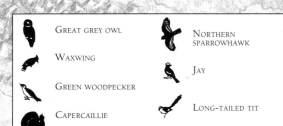

	GREAT GREY OWL		NORTHERN SPARROWHAWK
	WAXWING		JAY
	GREEN WOODPECKER		LONG-TAILED TIT
	CAPERCAILLIE		

Tail is longer than the body — no other woodland bird has such a long tail.

LONG-TAILED TIT

The tiny, restless long-tailed tit flits about in flocks, feeding on insects, spiders, and seeds. In spring, it builds an elaborate nest of moss, cobwebs, and hair, lined with thousands of feathers to keep its young warm. The nest is so small that adult birds have to fold their tails over their heads to fit inside it.

Long-tailed tit
(Aegithalos caudatus)
Length: 14 cm (6 in)

Large circles of feathers on face collect sounds rather like radar dishes.

GREAT GREY OWL

This huge owl uses its incredibly sharp hearing to detect voles on the forest floor. Even in winter, it can hear them run through tunnels beneath deep snow. The great grey owl defends its nest fiercely and will sometimes strike people if they get too close. The owlets leave the nest when they are 3-4 weeks old but take a week or so longer to learn how to fly.

Great grey owl
(Strix nebulosa)
Length: up to 84 cm (2 ft 7 in)
Wingspan: over 1.5 m (5 ft)

During his courtship display the male capercaillie fans out his tail, points his bill in the air, and puffs out his throat feathers.

Capercaillie
(Tetrao urogallus)
Length: male 87 cm (2 ft 10 in); female 60 cm (2 ft)

Enormous pine trees are typical of the coniferous forests of northern Europe, particularly in Scandinavia.

Lake Onega

Volga

Comb-like fringes on its toes may help the bird to walk on snow without sinking in.

CAPERCAILLIE

This bird lives in conifer forests, feeding on pine seeds and needles in winter and leaves, stems, and berries in summer. It nests on the forest floor. During his courtship display, the male challenges rival males with an extraordinary song, which ends with a popping and gurgling sound – like a cork being pulled out of a bottle and the drink being poured.

Tiny, red, wax-like blobs on the wings.

Waxwing
(Bombycilla garrulus)
Length: 18 cm (7 in)

Male has black and red "moustache"; female's moustache is all black.

GREEN WOODPECKER

This woodpecker is sometimes called the "yaffle", after its loud, laughing call. It has a large, dagger-like bill for probing ant hills or boring into tree trunks, and a very long tongue for licking up the insects hidden inside. It lives mainly on insects, but also eats fruit and seeds. During courtship, pairs of green woodpeckers spiral around trees.

Green woodpecker
(Picus viridis)
Length: 33 cm (13 in)

Green woodpeckers spend a lot of time on the ground, searching for ants.

Hawthorn berries are a favourite food.

WAXWING

The red tips on some of this bird's wing feathers look like sealing wax, which explains why it is called a waxwing. The waxwing lives in groups and chatters loudly in the breeding season. During courtship, male and female birds pass food from bill to bill. Its food is mainly the fruit and berries of woodland trees and shrubs.

The Mediterranean

IN SOUTHERN EUROPE and around the shores of the Mediterranean Sea, the climate is warmer and drier than it is further north. People have cleared away most of the forests that originally grew here, leaving small evergreen trees, thorny shrubs, heathers, and scented herbs in their place. During the long, hot summers, the air is alive with buzzing insects, which provide a rich food supply for warblers, bee-eaters, rollers, and other insect-eating birds. Large numbers of birds, such as storks, buzzards, and eagles, pass through the Mediterranean region as they migrate between Europe and Africa. The area also has some important marshland nature reserves, in particular the Camargue in France and the Coto de Doñana in southern Spain.

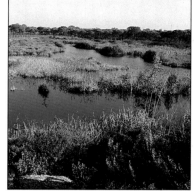

The lagoons of the Coto de Doñana nature reserve attract large numbers of water birds. The reserve has the largest heron colony in Europe.

The roller swoops down from a perch to catch insects.

European roller
(Coracias garrulus)
Length: 30 cm (12 in)

EUROPEAN ROLLER
All rollers are named after the male's rolling display flight: he flies up high then dives down, rocking from side to side and somersaulting through the air. The European roller eats mainly insects, but also hunts for lizards, snails, frogs, and other birds. In autumn it migrates south to Africa.

Golden oriole
(Oriolus oriolus)
Length: 25 cm (10 in)

GOLDEN ORIOLE
The woven, grassy nest of the golden oriole hangs below a forked branch like a hammock. It is a shy bird that spends most of its time hidden high in the tree-tops feeding on insects and fruit. The female grasps food in her sharp, stout bill to feed to her young. The golden oriole flies swiftly, and during courtship the male flies after the female in a high-speed chase.

The male is brightly coloured to attract the paler female.

The female does most of the nest building and takes care of the young.

HOOPOE
The hoopoe is named after its loud call, which sounds like "hoo-poo-poo". It walks and runs over the ground, searching for worms and insects with its thin, curved bill. If a bird of prey flies overhead, an adult hoopoe spreads its wings and tail flat against the ground and points its bill straight up, ready to attack the enemy. When it is excited, it raises the crest on its head.

Hoopoe
(Upupa epops)
Length: 28 cm (11 in)

The hoopoe flaps its rounded black and white wings rather like a butterfly.

Garonne

Rhône

ALPS

EUROPE

CARPATHIAN MTS

PYRENEES

Duero

Camargue
(See facing page)

APENNINES

Danube

BLACK SEA

COTO DE
DOÑANA

SARDINIA

M E D I T E R R A N E A N   S E A

SICILY

Euphrates

A T L A S   M T S

N O R T H   A F R I C A

0	250	500 km	
0	150	300 miles	

Hoopoe		Marsh harrier	
European roller		Golden oriole	
Northern shoveler		Purple heron	
Pied avocet			

The Camargue

The salty marshes and shallow lakes of the Camargue nature reserve formed where the River Rhône meets the Mediterranean Sea. Despite people, houses, and industry all around and aircraft flying overhead, large numbers of wading birds and water birds live there; still more pass through on their migration routes. Tens of thousands of swans, ducks, and geese visit the Camargue in winter from their breeding grounds in northern Europe and Siberia. The birds share out the available food by feeding in different places and on different types of food: stilts feed in shallow water while little egrets and purple herons prefer deeper water; herons catch fish, while spoonbills, flamingos, and avocets feed on small water creatures.

PURPLE HERON

The tall, slender purple heron has long toes to spread out its weight so that it can stalk over floating marsh plants easily, without sinking in. Its long legs allow it to wade into deep water where it fishes for food with its long, dagger-like bill. The purple heron usually nests in small groups of up to 20 pairs. The nests are hidden among reeds or rushes growing in shallow water. It is about six weeks before the young are able to fly away from the nest. When alarmed, the purple heron crouches with its bill pointing straight up. This pose, along with the stripes on its neck, make it hard to see among the reeds.

Northern shoveler
(*Anas clypeata*)
Length: 52 cm (1 ft 8 in)

The male is more colourful than the female.

Male

Big, shovel-like bill for filtering food from water.

NORTHERN SHOVELER

This bird gets its name from its shovel-shaped bill. At first, the chick has a normal bill, but this alters as it grows up. The adult shoveler sucks water into its wide bill and then pushes it out of the sides. Fine "combs" on the inside edges of the bill trap tiny floating animals and plants from the water as it flows over them.

Marsh harrier
(*Circus aeruginosus*)
Length: up to 56 cm
(1 ft 10 in)

Wings held in shallow V-shape to glide and soar over marshes.

MARSH HARRIER

As it glides and flaps slowly over reed beds and grassland, the marsh harrier searches for frogs, fish, small mammals, birds, and insects to eat. The female and her young stay on the nest, hidden among reeds and marsh plants. When the male brings food to the nest, the female flies up and catches it in mid-air. They also pass food in this way during courtship.

Females are larger than males, and female marsh harriers are the biggest of all harriers.

Very sharp, pointed bill to grab fish and frogs.

Purple heron
(*Ardea purpurea*)
Length: up to 90 cm (3 ft)

The heron is a shy bird, which it is hard to see until it takes off, usually making a squawking noise.

Greater flamingos feed on plants and small animals in the shallow waters of the Camargue. Three-quarters of all the flamingo chicks in the Mediterranean region hatch here.

PIED AVOCET

The pointed, upturned bill of the pied avocet sweeps through water, or the soft mud beneath it, in search of food, such as worms and small water creatures. Avocets prefer to nest on islands, where their young are safer from attack. They usually nest in large colonies so they can join forces against enemies.

Pied avocet
(*Recurvirostra avosetta*)
Length: 43 cm (17 in)

Long legs and long bill for feeding in deep water.

Coastal Areas

EUROPE'S JAGGED, IRREGULAR coastline provides many nesting places for seabirds. Millions come ashore in the summer to lay their eggs and raise their young on cliff ledges, burrows on cliff tops, beaches, and islands. Sea breezes along the coast help with take-off and landing. Although steep cliffs are dangerous for young birds, it is harder for enemies to reach them. There is also safety in numbers. Many seabirds crowd together in huge, noisy, smelly colonies made up of thousands of birds. Different species, such as guillemots, kittiwakes, gannets, and fulmars, may nest together on the same cliff. Each nests at a different level. In this way they share out the small amount of space available. Unlike land birds, seabirds do not need a large feeding area or territory on land to gather food for their chicks. They feed mainly out at sea so they can nest close together on land.

Large, powerful wings for gliding and soaring.

Long, strong legs for running and webbed feet for swimming.

Great black-backed gull
(Larus marinus)
Length: up to
79 cm (2 ft 7 in)

GREAT BLACK-BACKED GULL

This large gull is a fierce hunter, taking a wide variety of prey, from fish and seabirds to rabbits. In the summer breeding season, it attacks seabird colonies on the coast, gulping down a chick in a single mouthful. At other times of year, it scavenges for scraps on rubbish tips inland and around fishing ports and beaches.

LITTLE TERN

Bustling colonies of little terns gather on sandy beaches in summer. Members of the colony may help each other to dive-bomb enemies and drive them away. Young terns have to learn the best places to fish and how to dive headfirst into the water like their parents. At first their dives may be more like belly flops, but they soon learn. Unfortunately, the numbers of these terns have decreased because of people disturbing them.

Long, pointed wings beat quickly up and down.

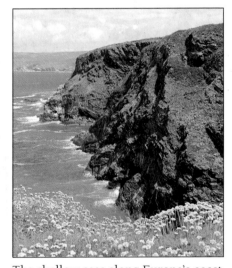

The shallow seas along Europe's coast are rich in food for the vast colonies of seabirds that nest there in summer.

Graceful and agile flight, sometimes hovering over the water.

Little tern
(Sterna albifrons)
Length: 23 cm (9 in)

Sharp, pointed bill for gripping fish.

GUILLEMOT

The guillemot, or common murre, spends a lot of time far out at sea. To catch fish, it dives below the surface, beats its wings rapidly, and steers with its feet. It comes to the coasts only to breed, forming dense colonies on cliff ledges. The birds are usually packed so close together that they touch their neighbours. The bird lays a single egg on to bare rock, without a nest. This means that one parent always has to stay and protect the egg and chick and keep them warm while the other parent goes off to sea to feed.

STORM PETREL

The storm petrel is the smallest European seabird. Fluttering above the water, it picks up small fish and plankton from the surface. A storm petrel will often follow ships to feed on the scraps thrown overboard and may shelter near ships during storms. It nests in colonies, mostly on isolated islands because it cannot defend itself easily.

Slim, hooked bill.

Streamlined shape helps bird to move fast through the water.

Guillemot
(Uria aalge)
Length: 41 cm (16 in)

Narrow, pointed bill for seizing fish.

As it feeds, the bird's legs dangle down so it looks as if it is "walking" on water.

Storm petrel
(Hydrobates pelagicus)
Length: 15 cm (6 in)

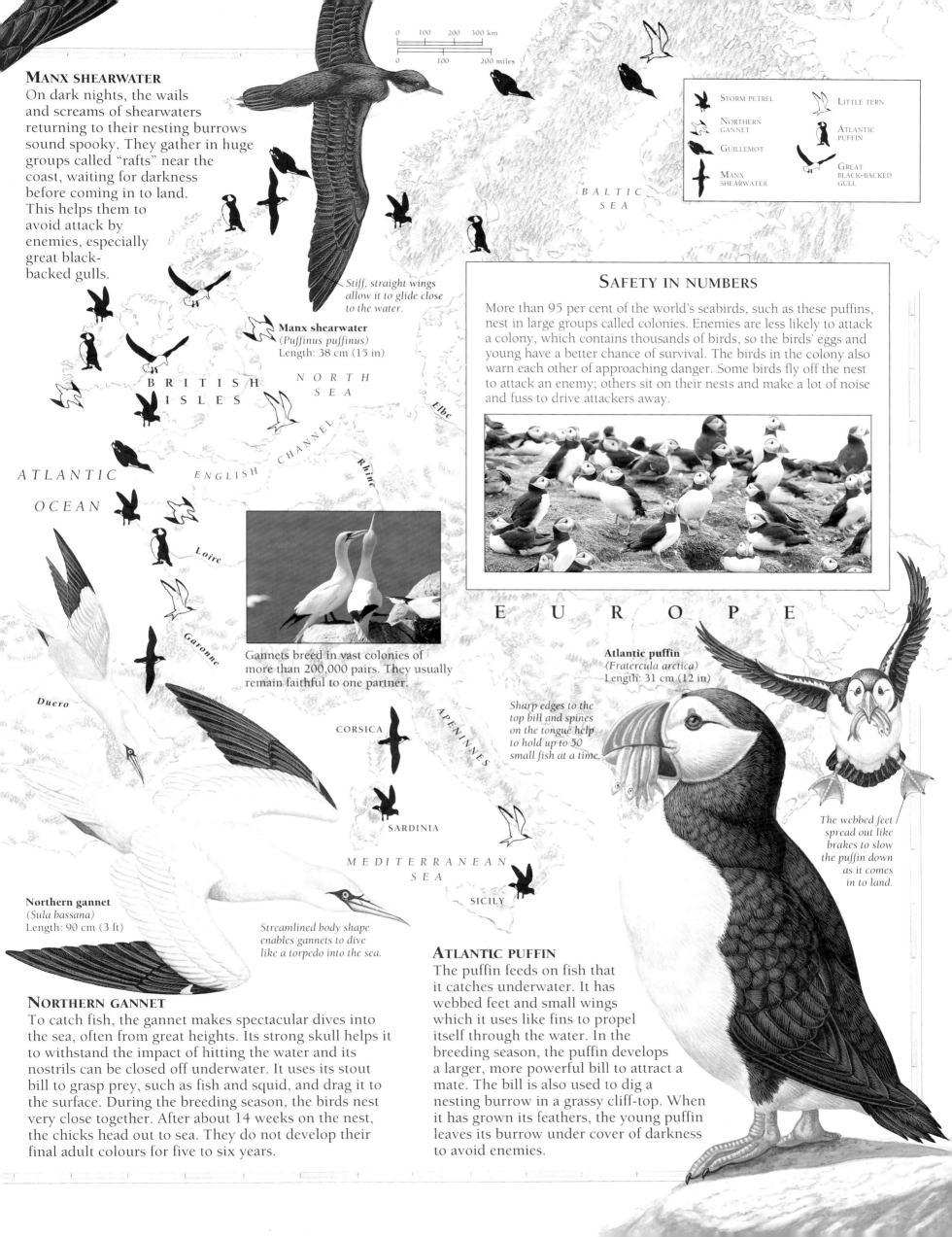

MANX SHEARWATER

On dark nights, the wails and screams of shearwaters returning to their nesting burrows sound spooky. They gather in huge groups called "rafts" near the coast, waiting for darkness before coming in to land. This helps them to avoid attack by enemies, especially great black-backed gulls.

Stiff, straight wings allow it to glide close to the water.

Manx shearwater
(Puffinus puffinus)
Length: 38 cm (15 in)

BRITISH ISLES

NORTH SEA

Elbe

Rhine

ATLANTIC OCEAN

ENGLISH CHANNEL

Loire

Garonne

Duero

BALTIC SEA

SAFETY IN NUMBERS

More than 95 per cent of the world's seabirds, such as these puffins, nest in large groups called colonies. Enemies are less likely to attack a colony, which contains thousands of birds, so the birds' eggs and young have a better chance of survival. The birds in the colony also warn each other of approaching danger. Some birds fly off the nest to attack an enemy; others sit on their nests and make a lot of noise and fuss to drive attackers away.

EUROPE

Gannets breed in vast colonies of more than 200,000 pairs. They usually remain faithful to one partner.

CORSICA

APENINNES

SARDINIA

MEDITERRANEAN SEA

SICILY

Atlantic puffin
(Fratercula arctica)
Length: 31 cm (12 in)

Sharp edges to the top bill and spines on the tongue help to hold up to 50 small fish at a time.

The webbed feet spread out like brakes to slow the puffin down as it comes in to land.

Northern gannet
(Sula bassana)
Length: 90 cm (3 ft)

Streamlined body shape enables gannets to dive like a torpedo into the sea.

NORTHERN GANNET

To catch fish, the gannet makes spectacular dives into the sea, often from great heights. Its strong skull helps it to withstand the impact of hitting the water and its nostrils can be closed off underwater. It uses its stout bill to grasp prey, such as fish and squid, and drag it to the surface. During the breeding season, the birds nest very close together. After about 14 weeks on the nest, the chicks head out to sea. They do not develop their final adult colours for five to six years.

ATLANTIC PUFFIN

The puffin feeds on fish that it catches underwater. It has webbed feet and small wings which it uses like fins to propel itself through the water. In the breeding season, the puffin develops a larger, more powerful bill to attract a mate. The bill is also used to dig a nesting burrow in a grassy cliff-top. When it has grown its feathers, the young puffin leaves its burrow under cover of darkness to avoid enemies.

0 100 200 300 km
0 100 200 miles

STORM PETREL	LITTLE TERN
NORTHERN GANNET	ATLANTIC PUFFIN
GUILLEMOT	GREAT BLACK-BACKED GULL
MANX SHEARWATER	

Africa

AFRICA IS THE SECOND LARGEST continent in the world. It is nearly three times as big as Europe, but about the same number of people live there. It was cut off from the other continents for millions of years and many of its birds – the ostrich, the shoebill, the secretary bird, as well as turacos, mousebirds, wood hoopoes, and helmet shrikes – are not found anywhere else in the world.

Africa is mainly a dry continent with large areas of desert and dry grassland. As a result, it has many land birds, especially seed-eaters.

The vast Sahara Desert forms a barrier to birds flying south across Africa, although millions of birds do make this journey every year to escape the European winter. The desert is spreading due to climate change and increased periods of drought. People have also caused the desert to spread at the edges by grazing too many animals there and reducing the vegetation cover. Africa's rich and varied bird life is also threatened by people cutting down forests, draining marshes and swamps, and building farms and cities.

CLIMATE AND LANDSCAPE

Most of Africa has a hot climate, with large areas that receive very little rain, especially the Sahara Desert in the north and the Namib and Kalahari deserts in the southwest. The wettest areas are near the Equator in the centre of the continent. Unlike other continents, Africa has few mountain chains. Generally, there are high, flat plains sometimes broken by a single mountain, such as Kilimanjaro in Tanzania, East Africa.

AFRICA ON THE MOVE

Africa has not always been in the position it is in today. Like all the other continents, it has gradually shifted around the Earth due to movements in the Earth's surface or crust. Africa was once joined to the other continents, but over millions of years, it has drifted away. African birds evolved into many unique species because they could not mix with birds from other continents.

About 130 million years ago Africa started to split away from the other continents and became a single continent. At that time Madagascar was still joined to mainland Africa. Later, it drifted away to become an island so the bird life there developed separately from that in Africa.

In the last 100 million years Africa has drifted towards Europe to its position on today's globe.

EUROPE

MEDITERRANEAN SEA

RED SEA

ARABIAN PENINSULA

Nile

ATLAS MTS

HOGGAR MTS

TIBESTI MTS

Lake Chad

A F R I C A

S A H A R A   D E S E R T

Niger

FACTS ABOUT AFRICA

Number of birds
About 1,700 species of bird live in Africa. Kenya has a particularly rich bird life, with more than 1,000 different species.

Deep lake
Lake Tanganyika is 1,435 m (4,708 ft) deep and is the second deepest lake in the world. Africa's largest lake is Lake Victoria, but this is only 81 m (266 ft) deep.

Longest river
The Nile is 6,670 km (4,170 miles) long and is the world's longest river.

Spectacular waterfall
The Victoria Falls on the River Zambezi drop 108 m (355 ft) over a ledge 1,700 m (5,580 ft) wide.

Biggest desert
The Sahara is the biggest desert in the world – it covers an area of about 9 million sq km (3,474,927 sq miles). The world's highest sand dunes occur in the Sahara. They can be up to 430 m (1,410 ft) high.

Colossal crack
The Great Rift Valley is about 6,400 km (4,000 miles) long and in some parts it is 35-60 km (22-37 miles) wide. It was formed about 25 million years ago when land slipped down between huge cracks, probably due to movements of the Earth's crust.

These storm clouds signal the start of the rainy season on the Tanzanian grasslands. Some African birds migrate from place to place within Africa, following the rains.

TYPICAL BIRDS
Here are just a few examples of typical birds from the most important habitats of Africa. These range from hot, dry deserts and open grasslands to warm, humid rainforests and rivers, lakes, and swamps. You can find out more about typical African birds and where they live on the next few pages.

Savannah
There are only two species of oxpecker in the world and they both live on the African savannah. Oxpeckers live on insects, which they take from the skin of grazing animals, such as this giraffe.

Islands
The cuckoo roller is one of many unique bird families that live only on the island of Madagascar. Others include the ground rollers, asities, and vanga shrikes.

Deserts
Birds find it hard to survive in a dry desert habitat, but sandgrouse can fly long distances to waterholes to find water and exist on a diet of dry seeds.

Rainforests
This pitta is a common bird of the rainforests. African rainforests used to be more widespread, but have shrunk as the climate became drier and people have cut the trees down.

Mountains
Birds of prey, such as this Verreaux's eagle, thrive in the African mountains where they can soar aloft on rising air currents and see their prey running on the bare ground below.

Hyrax

Marshes and swamps
Large numbers of fish-eating birds, such as this goliath heron, live and feed in vast tropical swamplands such as the Okavango Delta in southern Africa.

Lakes and rivers
Kingfishers, such as this pied kingfisher, are a common sight around African lakes and rivers, which are rich in food and nesting places.

ETHIOPIAN PLATEAU

INDIAN OCEAN

Lake Victoria

Lake Tanganyika

Lake Nyasa

GREAT RIFT VALLEY

Zambezi

MADAGASCAR

Congo

KALAHARI DESERT

NAMIB DESERT

ATLANTIC OCEAN

Forests and Mountains

STRETCHING ACROSS the centre of Africa is the second largest area of rainforest in the world. It grows in the tropical regions around the Equator, where the climate is hot and wet all year round. A variety of birds, such as hornbills, turacos, and pittas, thrive in this rich environment where there are plenty of leaves, fruits, and insects to eat and trees and bushes to nest in. There are also areas of rainforest growing on the lower slopes of the mountains in East Africa. On the higher slopes is a cold, misty world of grasses and giant plants, which is home to birds such as eagles and sunbirds.

The island of Madagascar off the east coast of Africa has areas of both mountain and rainforest, as well as deserts and grasslands. In this varied environment, which has been cut off from the rest of Africa for millions of years, many unique animals have evolved. These include several families of birds that are not found anywhere else in the world.

GREEN WOOD HOOPOE

These birds move around in a noisy family group, probing tree trunks and branches for insect grubs with their long, curved bills. Several times each hour, the birds perform a cackling display, which helps to keep the main group together. Up to 10 green wood hoopoes help each set of parents to gather food and defend the eggs and chicks. When the chicks grow up, they may become "helpers" for the adults who cared for them.

During the cackling display, the birds face each other, rocking to and fro and bowing low.

Tail is raised high in the air when the bird displays.

Green wood hoopoe
(Phoeniculus purpureus)
Length: 38 cm (15 in)

Sunbirds often feed on giant lobelia.

Scarlet-tufted malachite sunbird
(Nectarinia johnstoni)
Length: 15 cm (6 in)
Male's tail: up to 20 cm (8 in)

Both males and females puff out these red tufts to attract a mate.

Male's chest feathers turn green during the breeding season; at other times, they are brown. Tail feathers are long all year.

SCARLET-TUFTED MALACHITE SUNBIRD

This large mountain sunbird often perches on flowers to probe for sweet nectar with its long, thin, curved bill. It has strong feet and sharp claws for gripping slippery leaves. It also eats a lot of insects, holding them in the jagged edges near the tip of its bill. As it feeds, it helps to spread pollen from flower to flower. It has little flaps over its nostrils to stop pollen dust from getting up its nose.

Helmet vanga
(Euryceros prevostii)
Length: 31 cm (12 in)

Strong, hooked bill is used mainly for catching insects but the helmet vanga will also eat frogs and small reptiles, such as this chameleon.

HELMET VANGA

This bird belongs to a family of birds called the vangas, found only on the island of Madagascar. There are 14 species of vanga on the island. These probably evolved over millions of years from a single species of helmet shrike, which crossed over from Africa. Each of the species lives in a different habitat, so that there are enough nest sites and food to go round.

The yellow-billed hornbill hops from tree to tree, feeding on insects and fruit. Hornbills and turacos feed beneath the dense rainforest canopy out of sight of birds of prey flying above.

Legend/key box:

- Great blue turaco
- Helmet vanga
- African pitta
- Congo peafowl
- Trumpeter hornbill
- Green wood hoopoe
- Scarlet-tufted malachite sunbird

Map labels: Senegal · Niger · Blue Nile · White Nile · Red Sea · Congo · Kasai · Lake Victoria · Lake Tanganyika · Lake Nyasa · Lake Kariba · Zambezi · GREAT RIFT VALLEY · ATLANTIC OCEAN · KALAHARI DESERT · Limpopo · Orange River · DRAKENSBERG MTS · INDIAN OCEAN · MOZAMBIQUE CHANNEL · MADAGASCAR

0 250 500 750 km

0 250 500 miles

The casque on top of the bill is light and spongy inside. Males, like this bird, have larger casques than females.

Large, curved bill enables the bird to reach fruit in the trees and toss it into its mouth.

Trumpeter hornbill
(*Ceratogymna bucinator*)
Length: 66 cm
(2 ft 2 in)

Giant groundsels grow high on the African mountains. Sunbirds nest among their cabbage-like leaves.

Great blue turaco
(*Corythaeola cristata*)
Length: 76 cm (2 ft 6 in)

GREAT BLUE TURACO

Groups of up to 12 great blue turacos run and climb through the tree-tops. They feed on fruits, including berries that are poisonous to people. The nest is a flimsy platform of twigs built in a tall tree. When very young, chicks scramble about on the nest using tiny claws on their wings to keep their balance. After about four weeks, they leave the nest for good, but it is several days before they can fly.

TRUMPETER HORNBILL

The loud, wailing call of the trumpeter hornbill sounds like a child crying. Most hornbills have very unusual nesting habits. A pair build a round nest inside a hole in a tree then seal the opening, leaving the female inside. The male passes food to her through a narrow slit. This temporary prison protects her and her chicks from enemies.

African pitta
(*Pitta angolensis*)
Length: 18 cm
(7 in)

AFRICAN PITTA

The shy, tiny African pitta hops through dense undergrowth on the rainforest floor searching for slugs and insects. Although it is brightly coloured, it blends in surprisingly well with the leafy forest background. To threaten enemies, it crouches down with its wings spread and its bill pointing upwards.

Only males have this tuft of white bristles.

CONGO PEAFOWL

This unusual bird is the only true African pheasant – all the others originally came from Asia. Unlike other pheasants, such as the common peafowl (peacock), the Congo peafowl has a short tail. It lives on the rainforest floor, feeding on fruits and insects. Both parents probably help to take care of the eggs and young.

Both males and females have bright, shiny feathers.

Congo peafowl
(*Afropavo congensis*)
Length: 71 cm
(2 ft 4 in)

The Savannah

THE DRY, GRASSY PLAINS of the savannah provide food for a variety of seed- and insect-eating birds. Some of these birds depend on the mammals of the grasslands for their food. Oxpeckers, for instance, cling to giraffes, zebras, rhinos, and other animals with their sharp claws and snap up their ticks and other blood-sucking parasites. Vultures and marabou storks help to clean up the carcasses left by lions and other big cats.

In some parts of the savannah, trees, such as the flat-topped acacias, can be used as nest sites by birds such as weavers, starlings, or rollers. Other small birds hide their nests on the ground. The savannah has a wet season and a dry season. Birds tend to raise their young after the rains when the grasses are green and lush and there is plenty of food. Savannah bird life is increasingly threatened by people who live on and farm the remaining grasslands.

Hooked bill for tearing flesh from food.

Martial eagle
(Polemaetus bellicosus)
Length: 83 cm (2 ft 8 in)

Very strong, curved talons to kill prey.

MARTIAL EAGLE
This is the largest and most powerful eagle in Africa. A female may have a wingspan of 2.6 m (8 ft 5 in). This eagle either swoops down from great heights at high speed to attack its prey or lies in wait to ambush prey from a branch. The martial eagle builds its nest in tall trees. Females usually lay just one egg.

Masai ostrich
(Struthio camelus)
Length: 2.5 m (8 ft 2 in)
Height: up to 2.5 m
(8 ft 2 in)

SECRETARY BIRD
This bird was so named because its crest made it look like an old-fashioned secretary with a quill pen stuck behind his ear. It feeds on small mammals, insects, and some birds and their eggs. It can also kill snakes. The secretary bird snaps up small animals in its sharp bill but kills larger ones by stamping on them. During courtship, the birds fly up high making strange calls. The nest is a platform of sticks, which is built in the top of a tree.

The head crest is often raised while the bird is hunting.

Ostriches are the only birds with two toes on each foot.

Strong legs and toes, enable it to run at up to 70 kph (43 mph).

MASAI OSTRICH
It is impossible to look an ostrich in the eye unless you are incredibly tall. It is the largest and tallest bird alive today. It strides effortlessly across the savannah searching for leaves, seeds, and insects with its sharp eyes. The male makes a nest by scraping a hollow in the ground. Several females lay their eggs in one nest.

Secretary bird
(Sagittarius serpentarius)
Length: 1.5 m (5 ft)

Long legs enable it to walk easily through the tall grasses.

VULTURES

Soaring above the African grasslands, white-backed vultures like these keep a sharp look-out for dead animals to feed on. Their bare heads and necks allow them to feed without getting their feathers dirty. After a meal, vultures always clean their feathers well to keep them in good condition for flying.

VILLAGE WEAVER

Village weavers live in flocks and build their nests together so that they are safer from attack. There may be as many as 100 nests in one tree. The male builds the nest from strips of grass which he weaves into a round ball. He starts by building a swing to perch on, then makes a ring shape and finally a round ball. To attract a female, a male hangs upside down from the nest, flicking his wings. If a female likes the nest, she lays her eggs there and raises her young by herself.

These village weavers' nests are at the tips of branches where enemies such as snakes cannot reach them.

PARADISE WHYDAH
MARTIAL EAGLE
GREATER HONEYGUIDE
VILLAGE WEAVER
MASAI OSTRICH
SOUTHERN CARMINE BEE-EATER
SECRETARY BIRD

D E S E R T

A F R I C A

Nile

Lake Chad

Congo

A T L A N T I C   O C E A N

Zambezi

Paradise whydah
(Vidua paradisaea)
Length: 13 cm (5 in)

The weaver uses long, green grass stems to make the nest and loops and knots them together, rather like basket weaving.

The male holds his two short, wide tail feathers up above his long tail feathers during his display flights.

Village weaver
(Ploceus cucullatus)
Length: 18 cm (7 in)

Male village weavers may steal green grass from each other's nests.

PARADISE WHYDAH

To impress a female or warn off rivals, the male paradise whydah shows off his remarkable tail. The whydah does not take care of its young. Instead, the female lays her eggs in the nests of melba finches. Young whydahs have the same colours inside their mouths as young finches and also copy their calls and behaviour. This makes the foster parents feed the whydah chicks as if they were their own.

The female is a dull brown.

In the breeding season, the male paradise whydah grows tail feathers up to 28 cm (11 in) long.

Carmine bee-eaters live in colonies of hundreds of birds. They dig burrows in the soil, often in sandy vertical banks.

GREATER HONEYGUIDE

The honeyguide leads people or honey badgers to bees' nests. Once the "helper" opens up the nest, the birds eat the grubs and honey. The female lays her eggs in the nests of other birds – one egg in each nest. The young honeyguide injures or kills the other young with a hook on its bill.

Honeyguides have very thick skin to protect them against bee stings.

Each bird has a special calling place where it often perches.

The central tail feathers are up to 12 cm (5 in) long.

Southern carmine bee-eater
(Merops nubicus nubicoides)
Length: 38 cm (15 in)

SOUTHERN CARMINE BEE-EATER

The carmine bee-eater may perch on the back of an ostrich, stork, goat, or sheep, snatching up insects disturbed by its feet. It also gathers near grass fires where it eats up the insects trying to escape from the flames. The bee-eater specializes in eating stinging insects. To get rid of the sting, it holds the insect tightly in its bill and beats and rubs it against a perch. Then it swallows the insect whole.

Greater honeyguide
(Indicator indicator)
Length: 20 cm (8 in).

Rivers, Lakes, and Swamps

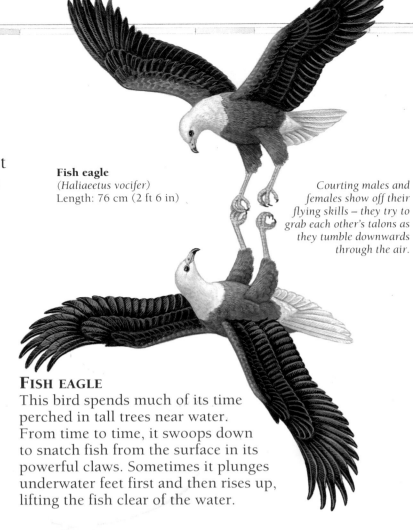

Fish eagle
(*Haliaeetus vocifer*)
Length: 76 cm (2 ft 6 in)

Courting males and females show off their flying skills – they try to grab each other's talons as they tumble downwards through the air.

AFRICA'S FRESHWATER HABITATS include great rivers such as the Nile and the Niger as well as vast swamps such as the Sudd and the Okavango Delta. These swamps, and the marshes that surround the great rivers, teem with life, especially fish. Large numbers of fish-eating birds live there, including herons, egrets, ibises, storks, and pelicans. Reeds and rafts of lilies growing in the warm, shallow waters also provide nest sites and safe places to feed.

In the east of Africa lies the Great Rift Valley. This long, narrow valley has formed where a section of the Earth's crust is slowly splitting, causing the land in between to sink. On the flat valley floor are many spectacular lakes. Birds from Europe and Asia use African lakes and swamps as resting places when they migrate across the continent.

FISH EAGLE
This bird spends much of its time perched in tall trees near water. From time to time, it swoops down to snatch fish from the surface in its powerful claws. Sometimes it plunges underwater feet first and then rises up, lifting the fish clear of the water.

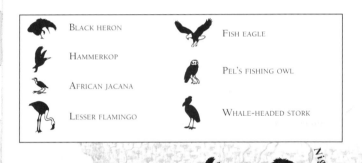

BLACK HERON		FISH EAGLE	
HAMMERKOP		PEL'S FISHING OWL	
AFRICAN JACANA		WHALE-HEADED STORK	
LESSER FLAMINGO			

Pel's fishing owl
(*Scotopelia peli*)
Length: 61 cm (2 ft)

Large eyes help the owl to see well in the dark.

PEL'S FISHING OWL
During the day, Pel's fishing owl hides away in trees near rivers and swamps. At night, it swoops low over the water, and catches fish in its powerful feet. Its legs and feet are bare so it has no feathers that could trail in the water and get wet and soggy. Unlike other owls, Pel's fishing owl does not have fringed feathers and soft plumage for silent flight; it does not need to fly quietly to sneak up on fish.

Feet have small spikes underneath to grip slippery fish or frogs.

A F R I C A

Lake Tana

GULF OF ADEN

Niger

Lake Volta

SUDD

White Nile

Lake Turkana

ATLANTIC OCEAN

Congo

Congo

GREAT RIFT VALLEY

Lake Victoria

INDIAN OCEAN

Lake Tanganyika

Lake Nyasa

Zambezi

OKAVANGO DELTA

KALAHARI DESERT

Limpopo

Orange River

Millions of flamingos flock to Rift Valley lakes, such as Lake Turkana, to feed on microscopic plants and animals growing there.

0	300	600	900 km

0	300	600 miles

The Okavango Delta is a vast swampy area where storks and pelicans live alongside hippopotamuses and buffaloes.

BLACK HERON

The black heron, or black egret, fishes for food in an unusual way. It spreads its wings out around its head to shade the water. The reason for this could be that the shaded area cuts out reflections on the surface of the water and makes it easier for the bird to see fish. Another explanation is that fish may swim into the dark patch thinking it is a safe shelter. When the heron spots a fish, it jabs its bill quickly into the water to grab a meal.

The bird makes an "umbrella" over the water with its wings for 2-3 seconds at a time by day or night.

Hammerkop
(Scopus umbretta)
Length: 50 cm (1 ft 8 in)

HAMMERKOP

This strange-looking bird is named after its hammer-shaped head. It builds a huge, roofed nest of twigs, grass, and mud, usually high in a tree near water. The nest is decorated with feathers, bones, snakeskins, and rubbish that people have thrown away. It is strong enough for a person to stand on the roof without falling in. Chicks are safe inside its thick walls while the parents find food.

Each nest takes from 1-6 months to build, but hammerkops often build several nests each year. No one knows why they do this.

Short tail and large wings for gliding and soaring easily.

Toes are partly webbed.

Black heron
(Egretta ardesiaca)
Length: up to 66 cm (2 ft 2 in)

Huge head to support the massive bill.

Large eyes help to spot fish and other prey in the water.

Hook at tip of bill helps to grab hold of wet, slippery food.

Long, thin bill for stabbing prey.

Whale-headed stork
(Balaeniceps rex)
Length: 1.2 m (3 ft 9 in)

LESSER FLAMINGO

Thousands of these flamingos flock to African lakes to nest and to feed on tiny water plants. To make sure the chicks get enough food, the parents produce a kind of rich "milk" in their crop – a pouch in the wall of the gut. The milk is bright red because it is dyed by pink pigment in the food they eat. Their feathers are pink for the same reason.

WHALE-HEADED STORK

Another common name for this bird is the shoebill because of its extraordinary shoe-shaped bill. The huge bill helps the bird to catch and hold its favourite food – lungfish. It also eats young crocodiles, turtles, frogs, and snakes. Parents sometimes collect water in their bills and pour it over their chicks in hot weather to keep them cool.

Lesser flamingo
(Phoeniconaius minor)
Length: 1 m (3 ft 3 in)

African jacana
(Actophilornis africanus)
Length: 28 cm (11 in)

Chicks make begging calls when they are hungry.

Long toes and claws spread out the bird's weight so it can walk on floating plants without sinking.

AFRICAN JACANA

These birds are also called lilytrotters. They run over floating plants pecking at the water and leaves to collect food. The male builds the nest, sits on the eggs, and takes care of the chicks, which is very rare for a male bird – female birds usually raise the young, often on their own.

Asia

ASIA IS THE LARGEST CONTINENT in the world. Much of northern, central, and southwest Asia has a cold, dry climate, with harsh deserts, dry grasslands, and frozen forests where few birds can survive. Many birds are forced to migrate south during colder seasons. The warm, rainy, tropical lands of Southeast Asia are, however, home to a spectacular variety of birds including pheasants, babblers, flycatchers, warblers, and thrushes. Some birds, such as the golden-fronted leafbird, the great argus pheasant, and the rhinoceros hornbill are not found anywhere else in the world.

To the west, Asia is joined to Europe and Africa and some of the birds are the same as, or similar to, birds in these continents. To the south, the islands of Southeast Asia form a series of stepping stones along which birds can move to and from New Guinea and Australia.

About half the people in the world live in Asia. They have made major changes to the land and plant life across the continent. Birds are increasingly threatened by the spread of cities and by forest destruction. Unless birds can adapt to an urban lifestyle, they have nowhere to live when their natural homes are destroyed.

INDIA ON THE MOVE

Over millions of years, continental drift has caused India to move into different positions on the globe.
About 200 million years ago, India was joined on to Africa, Australia, and Antarctica. But it split away on its own and slowly began to drift northwards towards Asia (right).

About 60-40 million years ago, India crashed into Asia, pushing up land from under the sea to create the gigantic folds of land that form the Himalayan Mountains. India is still pushing into Asia at a rate of about 1 km (0.6 miles) every 100,000 years.

CLIMATE AND LANDSCAPE

The great Asian mountain chains, such as the Karakoram, Pamirs, and Himalayas, cut across Asia from east to west, separating the warmer, wetter lands of India and Southeast Asia from the cooler, drier lands of central Asia. Southeast Asia consists mainly of thousands of islands, many of which were formed by volcanoes erupting through the seabed.

Many Southeast Asian islands, such as these in Indonesia, have a monsoon climate, with heavy rain in summer and cooler, drier winters. Seasons are altered by strong winds.

AMAZING BIRDS OF ASIA

Loudest woodpecker
This enormous woodpecker can be heard hammering at tree trunks from up to 1.8 km (1.12 miles) away.

Black woodpecker
(Dryocopis martius)

Most chatty bird
The hill mynah is the world's most talkative caged bird.

Heaviest head
The helmeted hornbill has a solid ivory casque on top of its bill, which gives it the heaviest bill of any bird.

Biggest tail
The crested argus pheasant has the longest and largest tail in the world. A male's tail feathers can reach 1.73 m (5 ft 8 in) long and 13 cm (5 in) wide.

Quickest chicks
The chicks of the Cabot's tragopan are the quickest to fly after hatching. They grow all their flight feathers within 24 hours of hatching and can flutter up into the trees immediately.

Heaviest flier
The great bustard is the world's heaviest flying bird. Males can weigh up to 18 kg (40 lb) – as much as a small child.

Great bustard
(Otis tarda)

FACTS ABOUT ASIA

Highest mountains
The Himalayas are the world's highest mountain range and contain the highest point on Earth – Mount Everest – which reaches 8,848 m (29,028 ft).

Number of birds
About 1,900 species of bird live in tropical mainland Asia, Sri Lanka, Sumatra, Java, Borneo, Taiwan, Hainan, and the Philippines. Over 300 birds breed in the Philippines alone.

Biggest forest
The conifer forests of northern Asia, called the taiga, cover more than 12 million sq km (4.5 million sq miles) from Scandinavia in the west to the coast of the Pacific Ocean in the east. The taiga is the largest forest in the world.

Most volcanoes
Java in Indonesia has about 50 volcanoes. Mount Bromo (below) is the biggest of them. Volcanic soils cover about 16 per cent of Japan.

Largest delta
The delta of the Ganges and Brahmaputra rivers in India covers an area of 60,000 sq km (23,000 sq miles).

Deepest lake on Earth
Lake Baikal in Siberia is the largest lake in Asia. It is 1,637m (5,317 ft) deep and contains one-fifth of all the fresh water on Earth.

Highest rainfall
Cherrapunji in India has the highest rainfall in the world – 10,800 mm (425 in) in a year.

TYPICAL BIRDS

Here are just a few examples of typical birds from the most important habitats of Asia. You can find out more about typical birds and their habitats on the next few pages.

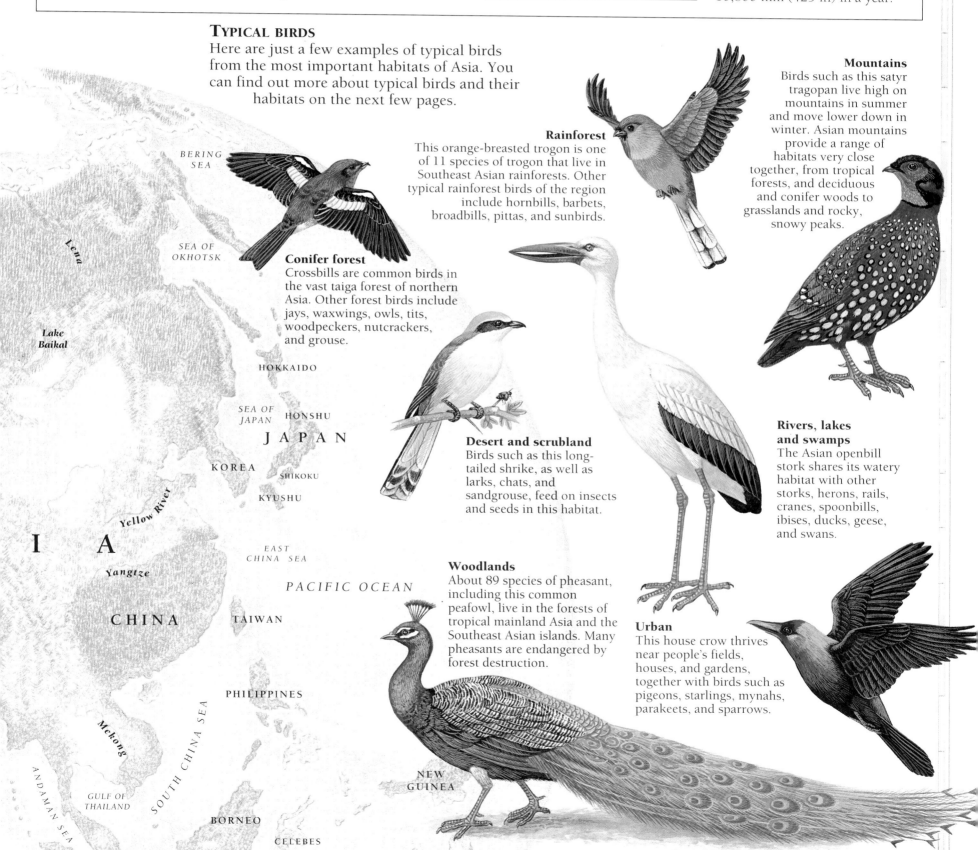

Rainforest
This orange-breasted trogon is one of 11 species of trogon that live in Southeast Asian rainforests. Other typical rainforest birds of the region include hornbills, barbets, broadbills, pittas, and sunbirds.

Mountains
Birds such as this satyr tragopan live high on mountains in summer and move lower down in winter. Asian mountains provide a range of habitats very close together, from tropical forests, and deciduous and conifer woods to grasslands and rocky, snowy peaks.

Conifer forest
Crossbills are common birds in the vast taiga forest of northern Asia. Other forest birds include jays, waxwings, owls, tits, woodpeckers, nutcrackers, and grouse.

Desert and scrubland
Birds such as this long-tailed shrike, as well as larks, chats, and sandgrouse, feed on insects and seeds in this habitat.

Rivers, lakes and swamps
The Asian openbill stork shares its watery habitat with other storks, herons, rails, cranes, spoonbills, ibises, ducks, geese, and swans.

Woodlands
About 89 species of pheasant, including this common peafowl, live in the forests of tropical mainland Asia and the Southeast Asian islands. Many pheasants are endangered by forest destruction.

Urban
This house crow thrives near people's fields, houses, and gardens, together with birds such as pigeons, starlings, mynahs, parakeets, and sparrows.

Map labels: BERING SEA, Lena, SEA OF OKHOTSK, Lake Baikal, HOKKAIDO, SEA OF JAPAN, HONSHU, JAPAN, KOREA, SHIKOKU, KYUSHU, Yellow River, EAST CHINA SEA, I A, Yangtze, CHINA, TAIWAN, PACIFIC OCEAN, Mekong, PHILIPPINES, SOUTH CHINA SEA, GULF OF THAILAND, ANDAMAN SEA, BORNEO, CELEBES, SUMATRA, INDONESIA, JAVA, NEW GUINEA, AUSTRALIA

The Himalayas

FROM THE FROZEN snow-covered peaks down to the hot forests on the lower slopes, the huge Himalayan Mountains provide a wide range of habitats for birds. At the top of the mountains, the bitterly cold weather and steep rocky slopes cause the death of many animals, so lammergeiers, vultures, ravens, and other birds that eat dead animals have a steady food supply. In the warmer summer months, flower meadows further down the slopes are alive with buzzing insects. Accentors and redstarts eagerly snap these up, while the pigeons and partridges that also feed in these high meadows prefer to eat shoots and bulbs.

Many birds spend the summer feeding and nesting high up the mountains, but fly down to the sheltered forests in the foothills for the winter. These forests are rich in fruits and seeds and teem with mynahs, babblers, and parakeets. Unfortunately, many Himalayan forests have been cut down for firewood or to make way for farms. With fewer trees to soak up the rain and keep the soil firmly in place, water pours down the mountains into the valleys, causing serious floods.

Bar-headed goose
(*Anser indicus*)
Length: 75 cm (2 ft 5 in)

Flocks of geese fly in formation so that the wind flows past them more easily and doesn't hold them back.

Lammergeier
(*Gypaetus barbatus*)
Length: 1 m (3 ft 3 in)
Wingspan: up to 2.7 m (9 ft)

BAR-HEADED GOOSE

These geese breed in central Asia and migrate over the Himalayas to spend the winter in India. They rest by day near rivers and lakes. At night they graze in fields of crops, so farmers often shoot them. As it flies from one feeding ground to another, the bar-headed goose makes a wild, musical honking sound.

LAMMERGEIER

The acrobatic lammergeier, or bearded vulture, glides and soars over the high mountain slopes, searching for skeletons that have been picked clean by its cousin, the griffon vulture. The lammergeier feeds on the marrow inside bones. The bird flies up to great heights and drops the bones on to rocks to smash them apart. It may drop one bone up to 50 times before breaking it. A lammergeier will return to the same site year after year to crack open bones, and occasionally tortoise shells, in this way.

Long, thin tongue shaped like a garden trowel for scooping marrow from bones.

Stiff, black feathers hang down like a "beard".

WALLCREEPER

The nimble wallcreeper climbs up sheer walls of rock, probing for insects with its curved, pointed bill. It often spreads out its wings to keep itself propped up while it searches. In summer, the wallcreeper moves high up the mountains, but in winter, it moves down to the shelter of the lower slopes.

Flutters its wings like a butterfly so it is also known as the "butterfly bird".

Wallcreeper
(*Tichodroma muraria*)
Length: 15 cm (6 in)

The male has a black throat in summer.

HIMALAYAN MONAL PHEASANT
WHITE-CHEEKED BULBUL
INDIAN HILL MYNAH
BAR-HEADED GOOSE
LAMMERGEIER
WALLCREEPER
HIMALAYAN SNOWCOCK

Brahmaputra
Ganges
INDIA
HIMALAYAS
Indus
HINDU KUSH
Indus

Himalayan monal pheasant
(*Lophophorus impejanus*)
Length: 70 cm (2 ft 3 in)

A male Indian common peafowl displays his magnificent feathers. Many other spectacular pheasants live in the forests of the Himalayas.

Indian hill mynah
(*Gracula religiosa*)
Length: 28 cm (11 in)

Short, strong legs for mountain climbing.

Male

Female's brown feathers help to camouflage her on the nest.

Female

HIMALAYAN MONAL PHEASANT

This pheasant lives in the forests and meadows of the Himalayas, moving up and down the mountains with the seasons. It uses its powerful, curved bill as a digging tool to uncover roots, bulbs, and insect grubs. To display to a female, the male raises his crest, fluffs out his shiny neck feathers, fans his tail, and droops his wings. In many areas, these pheasants are threatened with extinction caused by hunting.

Bright yellow face wattles (folds of skin) stand out against the glossy black feathers.

INDIAN HILL MYNAH

The noisy hill mynah lives in the tops of forest trees on the lower mountain slopes, feeding mainly on fruits and nectar. It makes a wide variety of whistling calls and is a brilliant mimic of the human voice. People have taken many of these birds from the wild to be kept as "talking" pets.

Flocks of birds, such as these snow pigeons, fly at very high altitudes across the snow-covered peaks of the Himalayas.

HIMALAYAN SNOWCOCK

The mottled colours of the Himalayan snowcock blend in well with the rocks and snow on the high mountain slopes. It eats all sorts of plant material, including roots, tubers, berries, shoots, and seeds, but it often has to search large areas to find enough to eat. In the breeding season, males make whistling calls to impress females.

Himalayan snowcock
(*Tetraogallus himalayensis*)
Length: 56 cm (1 ft 10 in)

White-cheeked bulbul
(*Pycnonotus leucogenys*)
Length: 20 cm (8 in)

The Himalayan species of this bulbul has a long crest.

WHITE-CHEEKED BULBUL

This lively bulbul lives as high up as 2,100 m (7,000 ft) in the Himalayas. It often perches on the tops of bushes, bowing, flicking its tail, and calling loudly. The white-cheeked bulbul is not frightened of people. It is an inquisitive bird that lives near villages and towns and sometimes goes right inside houses to steal food.

Short wings and a long tail are characteristic of bulbuls.

BAY OF BENGAL

INDIAN OCEAN

EASTERN GHATS

WESTERN GHATS

DECCAN PLATEAU

Godavari

Narmada

GULF OF KHAMBHAT

SRI LANKA

Irrawaddy

300 miles
450 km

45

Southeast Asia

BETWEEN THE SOUTHERN EDGE of mainland Asia and northern Australasia is an area of shallow seas dotted with thousands of islands. On the islands nearest to Australia and New Guinea, Asian and Australasian birds mix together. On more remote islands, such as the Philippines, many unique birds have developed away from contact with other species.

There are many volcanoes in Southeast Asia and some of the islands in this area are in fact the tops of giant underwater volcanoes. The rich volcanic soils and hot, humid climate in this region have encouraged the growth of lush rainforests. A huge variety of birds live in these rainforests, where there are lots of insects, fruits, and seeds to eat. Great numbers of birds often gather on the fruit-bearing trees, but they are well camouflaged and hard to see in the depths of the forest. Many people live in this region and much of the original rainforest has been cleared to make way for villages, towns, mines, and farms. This leaves the birds with fewer places to live and threatens the survival of many species.

Deep, hooked bill for ripping open prey.

Monkey-eating eagle
(*Pithecophaga jefferyi*)
Length: 95 cm (3 ft 1 in)

MONKEY-EATING EAGLE

This fierce eagle glides over the tree-tops or swoops down from a perch to catch its prey. It hunts monkeys and flying lemurs (called colugos), as well as small deer and large birds such as hornbills. The monkey-eating eagle is one of the rarest birds of prey in the world because of the destruction of its forest home. Only a few hundred of them survive in the wild.

Flying lemurs (colugos) are a favourite food.

Two very long feathers in the middle of the tail.

The male fans out his stunning wing feathers to impress a female.

HORNBILLS

Hornbills are named after the strange, horn-like growth, called a casque, which many of them have on top of their bills. It is made of a thin layer of skin and bone over a light "honeycomb" structure. No one really knows what the casque is for. It may help one hornbill to tell the sex and age of another, or it may make the bird's call louder.

Great Indian hornbill
(*Buceros bicornis*)
Bird has a large, yellow casque and a loud, roaring call.

Helmeted hornbill
(*Rhinoplax vigil*)
The only species of hornbill to have a solid casque, made of a substance like ivory.

Rhinoceros hornbill
(*Buceros rhinoceros*)
Casque turns up at the end like a rhino's horn.

Rufous-necked hornbill
(*Aceros nipalensis*)
This hornbill has no casque at all.

GREAT ARGUS PHEASANT

In the breeding season, the male great argus pheasant clears his own patch of space on the forest floor, removing every leaf, twig, and pebble. Then he struts up and down, calling loudly to attract a female. If one arrives, he dances in front of her, spreading out his long wing feathers, which are decorated with dazzling golden eyespots.

Great argus pheasant
(*Argusianus argus*)
Length: male (including tail) 1.9 m (6 ft 2 in); female 63 cm (2 ft 1 in)

Edible-nest swiftlet
(*Aerodramus fuciphagus*)
Length: 10 cm (4 in)

Nests made of saliva.

EDIBLE-NEST SWIFTLET

Thousands of these swiftlets nest in caves along the coasts or in tropical rainforests. Those that live in caves use cup-shaped nests made almost entirely out of their own saliva, which hardens like cement. The nests are stuck to the walls and roofs of the caves. People collect these nests to make "bird's nest soup", so they have become valuable.

SOUTHEAST ASIA

GULF OF TONGKING

ANDAMAN SEA

ANDAMAN ISLANDS

GULF OF THAILAND

SUMATRA

PHILIPPINES

SOUTH CHINA SEA

BORNEO

CELEBES

INDONESIA

JAVA SEA

JAVA

FLORES

TIMOR

TIMOR SEA

PACIFIC OCEAN

NEW GUINEA

INDIAN OCEAN

Mangrove swamps grow along the coasts and are rich in fish for birds such as storks and kingfishers to eat.

Brilliantly coloured trogons are found in forests throughout Southeast Asia. They feed mainly on large insects living among the leaves.

Monkey-eating eagle	Edible-nest swiftlet
Long-tailed tailorbird	Great indian hornbill
Great argus pheasant	Rhinoceros hornbill
Lesser green broadbill	Rufous-necked hornbill
Blue-crowned hanging parrot	Helmeted hornbill

0 200 400 600 km

0 200 400 miles

Long-tailed tailorbird
(*Orthotomus sutorius*)
Length: 12 cm (5 in)

Nest is built inside a cradle of leaves sewn together by the bird.

Long, sharp bill for making holes in leaves.

The male grows two long tail feathers in the breeding season.

LONG-TAILED TAILORBIRD

This bird gets its name from its remarkable nest, which it makes by sewing together one or more leaves on a bush or low tree branch. The tailorbird uses its bill as a needle to make a row of holes in the edges of the leaves. Then it pulls spider or insect silk, or cottony plant material, through the holes, one stitch at a time. The tailorbird builds its nest inside this "pocket" of leaves.

LESSER GREEN BROADBILL

The shiny green feathers of the lesser green broadbill blend in well with the leaves of its forest home. This makes it hard for enemies to spot. The broadbill moves slowly about the forests in small flocks searching for fruits, buds, and a few insects. As it feeds, it often makes whistling or bubbling noises, which sound like a frog.

The male is a brighter shade of green than the female and has black wing bars and neck spot.

Lesser green broadbill
(*Calyptomena viridis*)
Length: 20 cm (8 in)

Hanging parrot sleeps or rests upside down, with its body arched backwards.

Blue-crowned hanging parrot
(*Loriculus galgulus*)
Length: 12 cm (5 in)

BLUE-CROWNED HANGING PARROT

This sparrow-sized parrot flies through the tree-tops, feeding on nectar, flowers, fruits, and seeds. Like a woodpecker, it sometimes holds its tail stiffly against a branch or tree trunk to prop itself up. At night, the parrot hangs upside down from a branch like a bat. This may help it to hide from enemies that hunt at night.

Japan and China

MILLIONS OF PEOPLE live in crowded cities in the lowland and coastal areas of Japan and China, so there are few places left for birds to live. Some, such as the Okinawa rail and Japanese crested ibis, are close to extinction. But the mountains and forests inland remain home to many birds, especially pheasants and cranes.

The islands of Japan have been separated from mainland Asia for millions of years, and many birds have evolved into distinct Japanese species. The variety of birds in Japan is due partly to the different habitats, but also to the climate, which ranges from warm Kyushu in the south to cold Hokkaido in the north. In China, the forests of the southwest are a refuge for birds such as Temminck's tragopan and the golden pheasant. Northern China consists of harsh deserts and grasslands, but sandgrouse and bustards survive there.

STELLER'S SEA EAGLE

The Japanese call the spectacular Steller's sea eagle "the great eagle". Every winter, large numbers of these birds gather in the steep, wooded valleys of northeast Hokkaido. Here they are protected from the fierce winter winds at night and go out hunting for fish during the day. They swoop down to the surface of the sea to snatch fish in their powerful, curved talons. Steller's sea eagles also feed on the carcasses of sea lions and other dead animals.

Steller's sea eagle
(*Haliaeetus pelagicus*)
Length: male 88 cm (2 ft 11 in);
female 1 m (3 ft 3 in)

The male has bright red patches around his eyes.

Both male and female mikado pheasants have long tails.

Mikado pheasant
(*Syrmaticus mikado*)
Length: male 88 cm (2 ft 11 in);
female 53 cm (1 ft 9 in)

Nest woven from pieces of grass, leaves, lichens, and moss.

PENDULINE TIT

The tiny penduline tit lives in reed marshes and nests in trees, usually willows. It builds an amazing hanging nest which looks like a woolly purse. Both male and female birds weave the nest, which takes about two weeks to finish. The female lays seven or eight eggs in the nest and the young birds stay in it for two to three weeks after they hatch.

Penduline tit
(*Remiz pendulinus*)
Length: 11 cm (4 in)

Pointed bill for poking into bark and find insects to eat.

Japanese white-eye
(*Zosterops japonica japonica*)
Length: 11 cm (4 in)

MIKADO PHEASANT

This pheasant lives only on the island of Taiwan. It feeds on berries, seeds, leaves, and insects in dense forests of oak, juniper, pine, and bamboo. In spring, the female lays about five to ten eggs, which take nearly a month to hatch into chicks.

HARLEQUIN DUCK

This duck lives by fast-flowing water. It spends the winter months on rocky shores but moves inland to rushing mountain streams in summer. The harlequin duck is a strong swimmer. It is quite at home in strong water currents and can even shoot rapids. It makes a shrill, whistling call, which can easily be heard above the loud noise of the water.

JAPANESE WHITE-EYE

This white-eye lives on the Japanese island of Honshu. It flies from tree to tree in flocks, searching for insects, seeds, buds, and fruit. In summer, the white-eye soaks up nectar from flowers with the brush-like tip of its tongue. In winter, it often visits people's gardens to feed on seeds and fruit.

Harlequin duck
(*Histrionicus histrionicus*)
Length: up to 48 cm (1 ft 7 in)

The male grows these colourful feathers to impress a female during the breeding season.

Map labels

0 250 500 750 km
0 250 500 miles

Irtysh
Ob
ALTAI MTS

ASIA

HINDU KUSH
Indus
KUNLUN SHAN
PLATEAU OF TIBET
HIMALAYAS
Ganges
Brahmaputra
INDIA

ARABIAN SEA
BAY OF BENGAL

Salween
Mekong

CHINA
Yellow River
Yangtze

EAST CHINA SEA

KOREA
SEA OF JAPAN
JAPAN
HOKKAIDO
HONSHU
SHIKOKU
KYUSHU
PACIFIC OCEAN

HAINAN
SOUTH CHINA SEA
TAIWAN
PHILIPPINES

Beautiful white whooper swans migrate to sheltered coastal areas of Japan for the winter. In spring they nest by freshwater pools.

Key box

Penduline tit
Steller's sea eagle
Mikado pheasant
Japanese white-eye
Harlequin duck
Pallas's sandgrouse
Red-crowned crane

PALLAS'S SANDGROUSE

This sandgrouse lives in the dry deserts and grasslands of northern China and central Asia. It feeds on the seeds and shoots of plants and flies long distances to reach water. While the chicks are too young to fly, the male brings water to them. He sits in water until his belly feathers are soaked. When he returns, the chicks drink from his feathers.

Pallas's sandgrouse
(*Syrrhaptes paradoxus*)
Length: up to 41 cm (16 in)

Long pointed feathers help this sandgrouse to fly fast.

"Chicks drinking water from male's feathers.

Red-crowned crane
(*Grus japonensis*)
Length: 1 m (3 ft 3 in)

A pair of cranes dance during courtship.

RED-CROWNED CRANE

Red-crowned cranes perform a spectacular courtship dance that involves leaping, bowing, and flapping their wings. They may even throw feathers or stones into the air. The dance helps a pair of birds to form a strong partnership. Cranes usually stay with the same mate all their lives and rarely dance once they have chosen a partner. Each pair defends a large breeding territory and calls loudly to tell other cranes to keep out.

Australasia

AUSTRALASIA IS MADE UP of Australia (the world's smallest continent) and the islands of New Zealand and New Guinea, together with thousands of smaller Pacific islands. Australasia has been cut off from the rest of the world for millions of years and many of the birds in the region are not found anywhere else. These include scrub-birds, lyrebirds, and the emu in Australia, bowerbirds in Australia and New Guinea, and the kiwis of New Zealand. Some birds that are common in other parts of the world are not found in Australasia, for example there are no pheasants, woodpeckers, or finches. A number of birds migrate to Australasia to escape bad weather at certain times of year – waders fly in from the north and seabirds from the south.

Since settlers arrived in Australasia about 200 years ago, they have cleared many of the forests and the sheep, cattle, and rabbits they brought with them have destroyed many bird habitats.

AUSTRALIA ON THE MOVE
Over millions of years, continental drift has moved Australia slowly northwards. About 100 million years ago, it was joined on to Antarctica. But about 50 million years ago, it split off and started to drift. For about the next 30 million years, Australia was isolated from the rest of the world and many of its unique birds evolved. By about 10 million years ago, it had drifted near enough to Asia for some Southeast Asian birds to move into northern Australia.

CLIMATE AND LANDSCAPE
The middle of Australia, called the outback, consists mainly of desert and has a hot, dry climate, but the southern coasts are cooler and wetter. A tropical climate, with warm, wet weather all year round, occurs in northeast Australia and in New Guinea. New Zealand is cooler, with a temperate climate. The seasons in this southern part of the world are opposite to those in the north. For instance, when it is summer in Europe, it is winter in Australasia.

AMAZING BIRDS OF AUSTRALASIA

Speedy sleeper
The spine-tailed swift flies at speeds of up to 100 kph (62 mph) and can sleep while flying through the air.

Strong scent
The male musk duck has a strange pouch of skin under his bill which he uses to impress a female during his courtship display. The bird's name comes from the musky scent it produces during the breeding season.

Australian pelican
(*Pelecanus conspicillatus*)

Longest bill
The Australian pelican has the longest bill in the world. It can be up to 47 cm (1 ft 7 in) long.

Biggest nest mound
The mallee fowl builds a "compost heap" to keep its eggs warm until they hatch. The nest mound can be up to 5 m (more than 16 ft) wide and 1m (3 ft 3 in) deep.

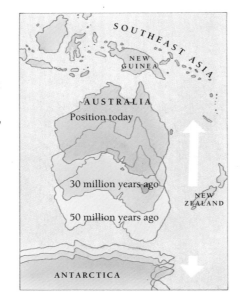

Musk duck
(*Biziura lobata*)

Curved bill
The wrybill of New Zealand is the only bird with a bill that curves to the right.

Biggest birds
The emu and cassowary are the second and third largest birds in the world, after the ostrich. Like the ostrich, emus, and cassowaries are too heavy to fly.

FACTS ABOUT AUSTRALASIA

Largest rock
Uluru (which used to be called Ayers Rock), is the world's largest free-standing rock. It lies in central Australia and is 6 km (4 miles) long and 2.4 km (1.5 miles) wide. It towers 348 m (1,143 ft) high above the desert floor.

Number of birds
More than 1,730 species of bird live in Australasia. About 60 per cent of the birds that breed in Australia do not occur anywhere else in the world.

Longest river
The Murray-Darling is the largest river system in Australia – it is about 3,750 km (2,330 miles) long.

Largest coral reef
The Great Barrier Reef, off the northeast coast of Australia, is the largest living structure on Earth. It stretches down the coast for over 2,000 km (1,243 miles).

Highest geyser in the region
The Pohutu geyser, in the volcanic region of New Zealand's North Island, is a violent jet of steam and water that shoots out of the ground reaching heights of 30 m (100 ft).

Least people
Fewer people live in Australasia than any other part of the world, except Antarctica. In Australia and New Zealand, sheep and cattle outnumber people by more than 10 to 1.

Flattest continent
Australia is the flattest continent. Almost two-thirds of its land surface is only 300-600 m (1,000-2,000 ft) above sea level.

Largest lake
The largest lake in the continent is Lake Eyre in Australia. The lake is often dry, but can cover an area of 8,900 sq km (3,436 sq miles) when flooded.

BORNEO   CELEBES

N E W
G U I N E A

INDONESIA

JAVA

ARAFURA
SEA

TIMOR
SEA

C O R A L   S E A

INDIAN
OCEAN

GREAT SANDY
DESERT

A U S T R A L I A

GIBSON
DESERT

SIMPSON
DESERT

GREAT VICTORIA
DESERT

Darling

GREAT DIVIDING RANGE

NORTH ISLAND

TASMAN
SEA

N E W   Z E A L A N D

GREAT AUSTRALIAN BIGHT

SOUTH ISLAND

SOUTHERN
OCEAN

TASMANIA

The outback of Australia consists of dry grassland and desert. This is partly due to the Great Dividing Range in the east, which stops moist winds from the Pacific Ocean reaching the middle of the continent.

Eucalyptus woodlands
The nectar and pollen of eucalyptus trees provides food for birds such as this rainbow lorikeet and many species of honeyeater, while parrots eat the seeds.

TYPICAL BIRDS

Here are just a few examples of typical birds from the most important habitats of Australasia. These range from rainforests, drier eucalyptus woodlands and grasslands, to deserts, scrubland, lakes, rivers, and swamps. You can find out more about the birds of Australasia on the next few pages.

Rainforests
There are 37 species of birds of paradise, such as this Count Raggiana's, living in New Guinea's lush rainforests. Four more species live in Australia's rainforests.

Swamps
Birds such as the brolga nest in swamps, which provide shelter from predators and are a source of food such as fish. Other swamp birds include bitterns, egrets, herons, and ibises.

Scrublands
Butcherbirds, such as this grey butcherbird, bell magpies, and currawongs all belong to the same family, which is found only in the scrublands of Australia and New Guinea.

Lakes and rivers
Waterbirds, such as this black swan, as well as ducks, and geese, feed and nest in freshwater habitats.

Deserts
Chats, such as this orange chat, and some parrots and pigeons manage to survive in deserts. They wander over large areas to find water and nest after rainfall, when insects start to hatch and plants grow.

Islands
The brown kiwi is just one of many unique flightless birds that live only on the islands of New Zealand. They evolved at a time when there were few enemies to fly away from.

Woodland and Desert

MOST OF AUSTRALIA HAS a dry climate. Vast areas in the middle of the continent are covered by hot desert, grassland, and scrubland, called the bush or outback. Some birds, such as chats, grasswrens, parrots, and pigeons, manage to find enough seeds and fruits to survive there, although they have to fly long distances to find water. Birds of prey can also live here by feeding on the many desert reptiles and small marsupials (mammals with pouches).

In the southeast and southwest of Australia are woodlands where a variety of eucalyptus trees grow. Here the climate is generally cooler and wetter. Marshes sometimes form during the rainy season, providing food and nesting places for ibises, pelicans, black swans, and ducks. Honeyeaters and lorikeets feed on the nectar and pollen in the eucalyptus trees and in flowering shrubs, such as grevilleas and banksias. Parrots use their strong bills to crack open seeds. As they feed, the birds help to pollinate the flowers and spread their seeds. Birds that feed on insects also find a rich supply of food on the leaves and bark of the eucalyptus trees.

Sharp, pointed bill for stabbing reptiles, such as this snake.

Laughing kookaburra
(*Dacelo novaeguineae*)
Length: 45 cm (18 in)

LAUGHING KOOKABURRA
This giant member of the kingfisher family is named after its loud hooting and chuckling call. This tells other birds to keep out of its territory. Several birds may join in the laughter, usually in the early morning or late afternoon. The laughing kookaburra is also called the "bushman's clock" because it wakes people in the bush up at dawn. It sometimes comes to town and city gardens to eat the food that people leave out for it, and has also been known to raid goldfish ponds.

WESTERN SPINEBILL
The western spinebill uses its needle-thin, curved bill to probe for nectar in flowers. Its long bill can reach inside tube-shaped flowers or push into stiff, brush-like flowers, such as banksias. It sometimes hovers in front of flowers to drink the nectar, soaking it up with a brush at the tip of its tongue. This spinebill also eats some insects and soft fruit.

Western spinebill
(*Acanthorhynchus superciliosus*)
Length: 15 cm (6 in)

A western spinebill feeds on nectar from the flowers of a red gum, which is a kind of eucalyptus.

A male brown honeyeater feeds on a banksia flower. As honeyeaters feed, they pick up pollen dust on their feathers and carry it to other flowers.

Splendid fairy wren
(*Malurus splendens*)
Length: 14 cm (5.5 in)

This bird often cocks its tail when perched on a branch.

Males have shiny, bright blue feathers in the breeding season. Females are much duller in colour all year round.

SPLENDID FAIRY WREN
Pairs of splendid, or banded, fairy wrens nests in small groups, with extra birds helping to feed and defend the young. The helpers may be young birds that have not yet left their parents and started to fend for themselves. They help their younger brothers and sisters to survive.

GREAT SANDY DESERT

MACDONNELL RANGES

GIBSON DESERT

A U S T R A L I A

SIMPSON DESERT

GREAT VICTORIA DESERT

Lake Eyre

Darling

NULLARBOR PLAIN

FLINDERS RANGES

Murray

CORAL SEA

GREAT DIVIDING RANGE

GREAT AUSTRALIAN BIGHT

GREAT DIVIDING RANGE

TASMAN SEA

SOUTHERN OCEAN

BASS STRAIT

TASMANIA

| 0 | 200 | 400 | 600 km |
| 0 | 200 | | 400 miles |

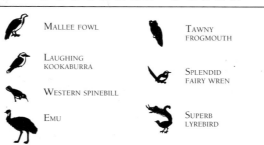

MALLEE FOWL

LAUGHING KOOKABURRA

WESTERN SPINEBILL

EMU

TAWNY FROGMOUTH

SPLENDID FAIRY WREN

SUPERB LYREBIRD

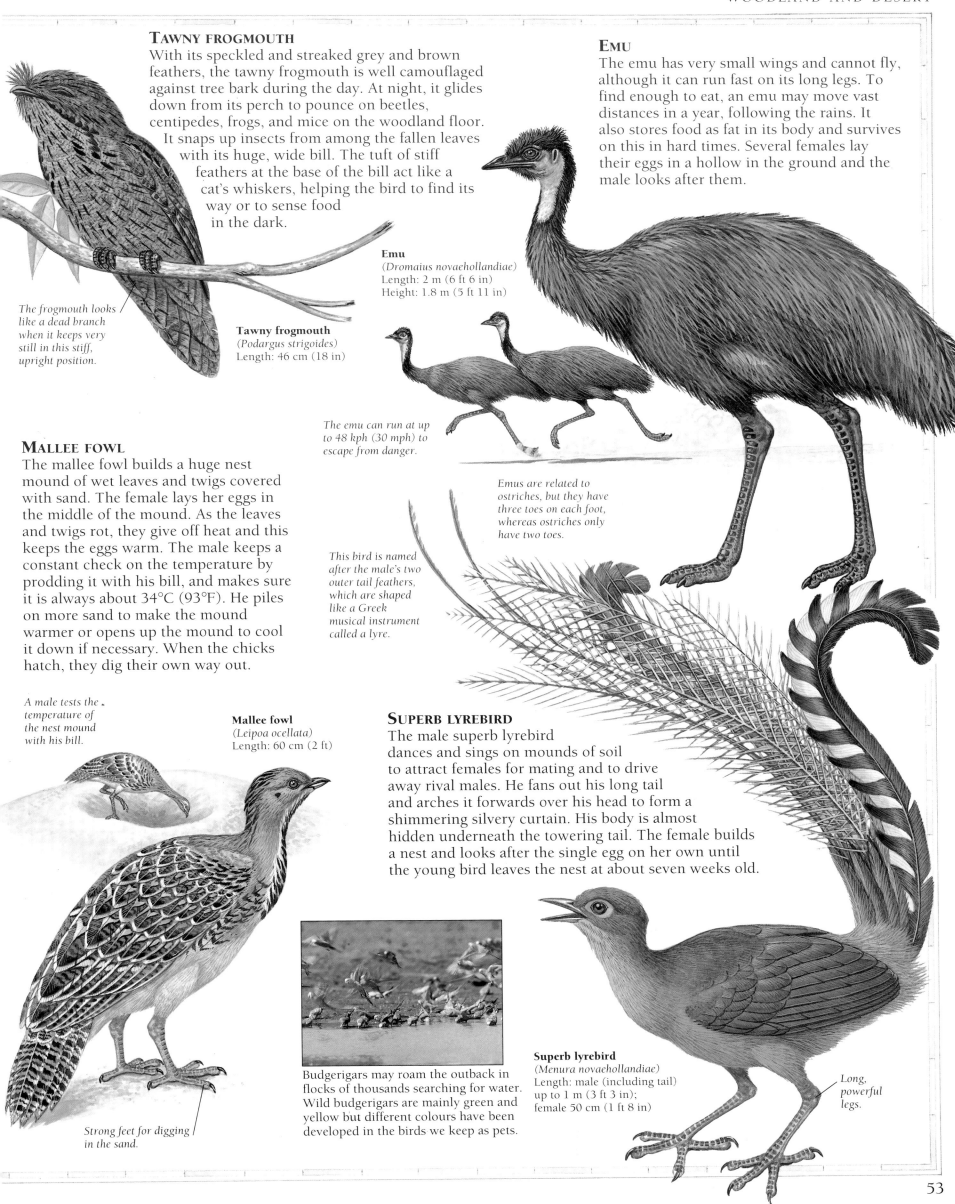

TAWNY FROGMOUTH

With its speckled and streaked grey and brown feathers, the tawny frogmouth is well camouflaged against tree bark during the day. At night, it glides down from its perch to pounce on beetles, centipedes, frogs, and mice on the woodland floor. It snaps up insects from among the fallen leaves with its huge, wide bill. The tuft of stiff feathers at the base of the bill act like a cat's whiskers, helping the bird to find its way or to sense food in the dark.

The frogmouth looks like a dead branch when it keeps very still in this stiff, upright position.

Tawny frogmouth
(Podargus strigoides)
Length: 46 cm (18 in)

EMU

The emu has very small wings and cannot fly, although it can run fast on its long legs. To find enough to eat, an emu may move vast distances in a year, following the rains. It also stores food as fat in its body and survives on this in hard times. Several females lay their eggs in a hollow in the ground and the male looks after them.

Emu
(Dromaius novaehollandiae)
Length: 2 m (6 ft 6 in)
Height: 1.8 m (5 ft 11 in)

The emu can run at up to 48 kph (30 mph) to escape from danger.

Emus are related to ostriches, but they have three toes on each foot, whereas ostriches only have two toes.

MALLEE FOWL

The mallee fowl builds a huge nest mound of wet leaves and twigs covered with sand. The female lays her eggs in the middle of the mound. As the leaves and twigs rot, they give off heat and this keeps the eggs warm. The male keeps a constant check on the temperature by prodding it with his bill, and makes sure it is always about 34°C (93°F). He piles on more sand to make the mound warmer or opens up the mound to cool it down if necessary. When the chicks hatch, they dig their own way out.

This bird is named after the male's two outer tail feathers, which are shaped like a Greek musical instrument called a lyre.

A male tests the temperature of the nest mound with his bill.

Mallee fowl
(Leipoa ocellata)
Length: 60 cm (2 ft)

SUPERB LYREBIRD

The male superb lyrebird dances and sings on mounds of soil to attract females for mating and to drive away rival males. He fans out his long tail and arches it forwards over his head to form a shimmering silvery curtain. His body is almost hidden underneath the towering tail. The female builds a nest and looks after the single egg on her own until the young bird leaves the nest at about seven weeks old.

Budgerigars may roam the outback in flocks of thousands searching for water. Wild budgerigars are mainly green and yellow but different colours have been developed in the birds we keep as pets.

Superb lyrebird
(Menura novaehollandiae)
Length: male (including tail) up to 1 m (3 ft 3 in); female 50 cm (1 ft 8 in)

Long, powerful legs.

Strong feet for digging in the sand.

Rainforests

THE BIRDS OF THE lush rainforests of northeastern Australia resemble those of New Guinea more than the rest of Australia. The two regions were joined for much of their history and have a similar warm, wet climate with rain all year round. Their rainforests are rich in fruit trees for birds to feed on but are rapidly being cleared to make way for houses, farms, dams, and mines.

New Guinea is the second largest island in the world, after Greenland. Its high mountains, deep isolated valleys, and lack of mammal enemies have allowed a huge variety of birds to evolve there, including the spectacular bowerbirds and birds of paradise. There are also more kinds of kingfisher in New Guinea than anywhere else in the world.

BOWERBIRDS

Bowerbirds are related to birds of paradise but the male birds do not have such colourful and elaborate feathers. Instead, they build "bowers" – shelters made out of twigs – and decorate them with colourful objects. Females choose to mate with the males that have the best bowers, then go off to build their nests safely hidden in the forest.

Satin bowerbird
(*Ptilonorhynchus violaceus*)
Length: 33 cm (13 in)

"Avenue" bower decorated with blue things.

MacGregor's gardener
(*Amblyornis macgregoriae*)
Length: 25.5 cm (10 in)

"Maypole" bower; bird has large orange crest.

Vogelkop gardener
(*Amblyornis inornatus*)
Length: 30 cm (12 in)

Complex "hut" bower; bird has no crest and feathers are a dull colour.

Pigeon flies up into trees and perches on branches to escape danger.

Victoria crowned pigeon
(*Goura victoria*)
Length: 66 cm (2 ft 2 in)

VICTORIA CROWNED PIGEON

This is one of the biggest pigeons in the world and is the size of a large chicken. Despite its size, this pigeon nests up to 15 m (49 ft) high in the trees. The male Victoria crowned pigeon bows his head during his courtship display to show off his splendid crest to the female. At the same time, he spreads his tail out, fans it up and down, and makes a booming call.

Rivers bordered by rainforest in northeastern Australia provide a very lush habitat for birds. This is in contrast to the dry, hot deserts at the centre of the continent.

DOUBLE-WATTLED CASSOWARY

This huge cassowary is the same height and weight as a small human being. It uses the tall, horny casque on its head to push aside the tangled forest undergrowth. Its long, hair-like feathers protect its body and stop it getting scratched. The double-wattled cassowary wanders around the rainforest searching for seeds, berries, and fruits to eat. Its survival is threatened by the destruction of its forest home.

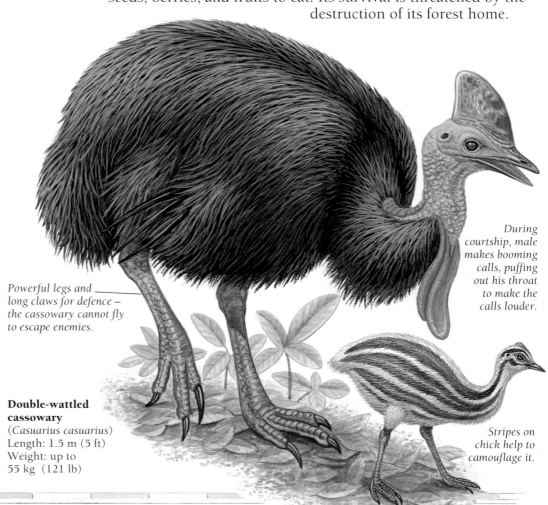

Powerful legs and long claws for defence – the cassowary cannot fly to escape enemies.

Double-wattled cassowary
(*Casuarius casuarius*)
Length: 1.5 m (5 ft)
Weight: up to 55 kg (121 lb)

During courtship, male makes booming calls, puffing out his throat to make the calls louder.

Stripes on chick help to camouflage it.

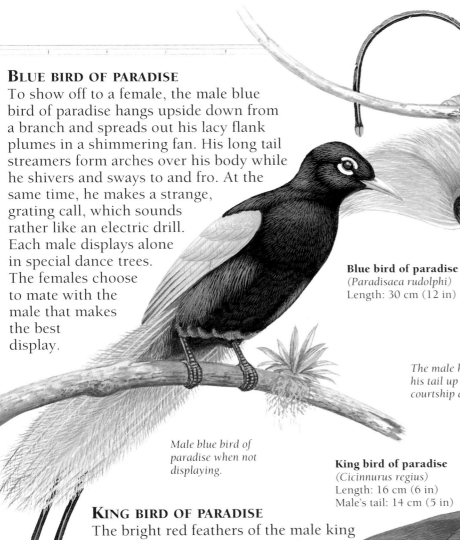

BLUE BIRD OF PARADISE

To show off to a female, the male blue bird of paradise hangs upside down from a branch and spreads out his lacy flank plumes in a shimmering fan. His long tail streamers form arches over his body while he shivers and sways to and fro. At the same time, he makes a strange, grating call, which sounds rather like an electric drill. Each male displays alone in special dance trees. The females choose to mate with the male that makes the best display.

Male displaying to a female.

Blue bird of paradise
(*Paradisaea rudolphi*)
Length: 30 cm (12 in)

Male blue bird of paradise when not displaying.

ECLECTUS PARROT

Male and female eclectus parrots are such different colours that they were once thought to be different species. Both have some green feathers for camouflage in the rainforest, but the female stands out more than her mate. She is the only female parrot to be brighter than the male. Eclectus parrots roost at night in groups of up to 80 birds. By day, they travel through the tree-tops, searching for fruits, nuts, nectar, and leaves to eat.

The male holds his tail up during courtship display.

King bird of paradise
(*Cicinnurus regius*)
Length: 16 cm (6 in)
Male's tail: 14 cm (5 in)

KING BIRD OF PARADISE

The bright red feathers of the male king bird of paradise contrast with the dull brown of the female. The female's colours help camouflage her while she cares for the eggs and chicks. She collects all the food she needs for herself and her chicks in the rainforest, leaving the male free for his stunning courtship displays.

Feet have a strong, vice-like grip on branches.

Male

Female

Eclectus parrot
(*Eclectus roratus*)
Length: 38 cm (15 in)

NEW BRITAIN

NEW GUINEA

| 0 | 250 | 500 km |
| 0 | 200 | 400 miles |

ARAFURA SEA

SOLOMON ISLANDS

CORAL SEA

PACIFIC OCEAN

GULF OF CARPENTARIA

A gang-gang cockatoo feasts on forest berries. This bird is known for its loud, creaky door-like screech.

GREAT SANDY DESERT

RED-BREASTED PYGMY PARROT

This unique parrot lives only on New Guinea and some of the nearby islands, where there are no woodpeckers. As it clings to tree trunks, this parrot uses its spiny tail feathers for support – just like a real woodpecker. It feeds on lichens and fungi and may also eat other plants and insects.

Red-breasted pygmy parrot
(*Micropsitta bruijnii*)
Length: 9 cm (3.5 in)

Stiff tail used as a prop.

VOGELKOP GARDENER	
SATIN BOWERBIRD	MACGREGOR'S GARDENER
DOUBLE-WATTLED CASSOWARY	ECLECTUS PARROT
RED-BREASTED PYGMY PARROT	KING BIRD OF PARADISE
BLUE BIRD OF PARADISE	VICTORIA CROWNED PIGEON

GREAT BARRIER REEF

AUSTRALIA

New Zealand

NEW ZEALAND CONSISTS mainly of two large islands – North and South Island. North Island has a warm, temperate climate with active volcanoes. South Island is colder, with glaciers, mountains, and beech forests.

New Zealand does not have a great variety of bird species. This is mainly due to its isolated position. It drifted away from the other landmasses millions of years ago as a result of continental drift. However, the few species it has are very unusual. This is because New Zealand had very few mammals when it drifted off on its own, so the birds there began to live like mammals, running about and nesting on the ground. Many birds, such as the kiwi and the takahe, stopped flying altogether because there were no mammal enemies to escape from. Unfortunately, these flightless birds later became easy prey for stoats and other mammals that people introduced to the islands.

Kea
(Nestor notabilis)
Length: 46 cm (18 in)

Long top bill for tearing into fruit, leaves, insects, and dead animals. The male's top bill is longer than the female's.

KEA

This is an unusual parrot that lives in much colder habitats than most parrots, sometimes even in snow. In summer, it lives in the mountains but it moves down to the forests on the coast in winter. The kea is named after the sound of its call, which echoes round the steep mountain-sides. Both parents take care of the young until they are ready to leave the nest after about 13 weeks.

LITTLE PENGUIN

The smallest penguin in the world lives around the coasts and islands of New Zealand. The little penguin, also known as the blue or fairy penguin, spends the day fishing at sea, but comes ashore at night. In the breeding season, little penguins pair up with the same mates at the same nest site year after year. They nest in a cave, among rocks or grass, or in a burrow.

Strong flippers and webbed feet for swimming fast underwater.

Little penguin
(Eudyptula minor)
Height: 40 cm (16 in)

NORTH ISLAND

TASMAN SEA

PACIFIC OCEAN

BAY OF PLENTY

EAST CAPE

RAUKUMARA RANGE

Lake Taupo

HAWKE BAY

0   50   100   150 km
0   50   100 miles

Rangitikei

RUAHINE RANGE

NEW ZEALAND

TASMAN MTS

COOK STRAIT

TARARUA RANGE

SOUTH ISLAND

TASMAN SEA

PACIFIC OCEAN

SOUTHERN ALPS

CANTERBURY PLAINS

Rakaia

Waitaki

STEWART ISLAND

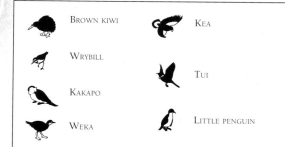

The bird's bill curves to the right, yet it holds its head to the left as it feeds.

Wrybill
(Anarhynchus frontalis)
Length: 20 cm (8 in)

WRYBILL

The wrybill is named after its strange crooked, or wry, bill which bends to the right at the tip, although no one is quite sure why this is. It is a type of wading bird related to the plover. The wrybill breeds on the stones and shingle of large river beds on South Island from August to December. The bird and its eggs are well camouflaged among the stones. In January it migrates to North Island.

Brown kiwi	Kea	
Wrybill	Tui	
Kakapo		
Weka	Little penguin	

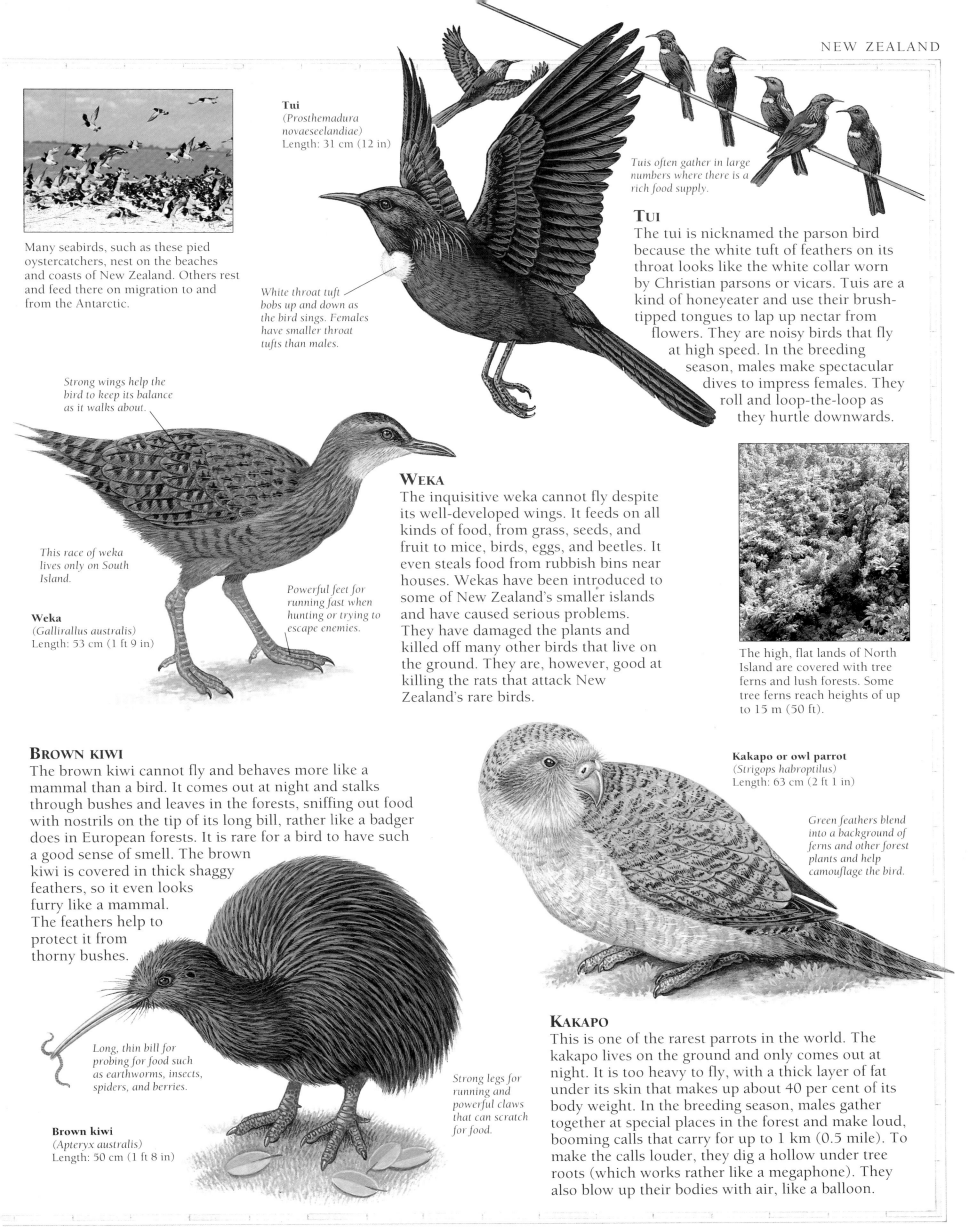

Many seabirds, such as these pied oystercatchers, nest on the beaches and coasts of New Zealand. Others rest and feed there on migration to and from the Antarctic.

Tui
(*Prosthemadura novaeseelandiae*)
Length: 31 cm (12 in)

Tuis often gather in large numbers where there is a rich food supply.

White throat tuft bobs up and down as the bird sings. Females have smaller throat tufts than males.

TUI
The tui is nicknamed the parson bird because the white tuft of feathers on its throat looks like the white collar worn by Christian parsons or vicars. Tuis are a kind of honeyeater and use their brush-tipped tongues to lap up nectar from flowers. They are noisy birds that fly at high speed. In the breeding season, males make spectacular dives to impress females. They roll and loop-the-loop as they hurtle downwards.

Strong wings help the bird to keep its balance as it walks about.

WEKA
The inquisitive weka cannot fly despite its well-developed wings. It feeds on all kinds of food, from grass, seeds, and fruit to mice, birds, eggs, and beetles. It even steals food from rubbish bins near houses. Wekas have been introduced to some of New Zealand's smaller islands and have caused serious problems. They have damaged the plants and killed off many other birds that live on the ground. They are, however, good at killing the rats that attack New Zealand's rare birds.

This race of weka lives only on South Island.

Weka
(*Gallirallus australis*)
Length: 53 cm (1 ft 9 in)

Powerful feet for running fast when hunting or trying to escape enemies.

The high, flat lands of North Island are covered with tree ferns and lush forests. Some tree ferns reach heights of up to 15 m (50 ft).

BROWN KIWI
The brown kiwi cannot fly and behaves more like a mammal than a bird. It comes out at night and stalks through bushes and leaves in the forests, sniffing out food with nostrils on the tip of its long bill, rather like a badger does in European forests. It is rare for a bird to have such a good sense of smell. The brown kiwi is covered in thick shaggy feathers, so it even looks furry like a mammal. The feathers help to protect it from thorny bushes.

Kakapo or owl parrot
(*Strigops habroptilus*)
Length: 63 cm (2 ft 1 in)

Green feathers blend into a background of ferns and other forest plants and help camouflage the bird.

Long, thin bill for probing for food such as earthworms, insects, spiders, and berries.

Brown kiwi
(*Apteryx australis*)
Length: 50 cm (1 ft 8 in)

Strong legs for running and powerful claws that can scratch for food.

KAKAPO
This is one of the rarest parrots in the world. The kakapo lives on the ground and only comes out at night. It is too heavy to fly, with a thick layer of fat under its skin that makes up about 40 per cent of its body weight. In the breeding season, males gather together at special places in the forest and make loud, booming calls that carry for up to 1 km (0.5 mile). To make the calls louder, they dig a hollow under tree roots (which works rather like a megaphone). They also blow up their bodies with air, like a balloon.

Antarctica

ANTARCTICA IS THE coldest and windiest place on Earth. Unlike the Arctic, which is an ocean surrounded by land, Antarctica is a huge area of land surrounded by ocean. Most of the land is covered by ice. Little rain or snow falls, so there is hardly any fresh water for birds to drink.

In these harsh conditions, only two landbirds manage to survive. Both are sheathbills – a type of bird related to a pigeon. The rest are seabirds, which have denser feathers than most land birds to keep them warm, and are better at flying in stormy weather. In summer, some of the ice around the coasts melts and millions of seabirds such as albatrosses, petrels, penguins, and shearwaters come ashore to lay eggs and raise their young. The Antarctic summer lasts for only about four months when it is light most of the time. During the winter, most of the birds leave Antarctica and roam widely over the southern oceans in search of food.

Kelp gulls fly slowly and often glide with their long wings stretched out.

KELP GULL

The huge kelp gull, or southern black-backed gull, is the only gull that stays in the Antarctic all year round. Kelp gulls are good at catching fish, but also eat shellfish, dead animals, and the eggs and young of other birds. They sometimes carry shellfish up into the air and drop them on to rocks to break them open. Both parents sit on the eggs for about a month to keep them warm and the chicks can fly when they are about 5-6 weeks old.

Kelp gull
(Larus dominicanus)
Length: 58 cm (1 ft 10 in)
Wingspan: 130 cm (4 ft 3 in)

Birds grow wispy crests in the breeding season.

IMPERIAL SHAG

The imperial shag has webbed feet for swimming. Its feathers soak up water, so its weight increases and it can sink and dive more easily. But it has to spread out its wings to dry after a swim. The imperial shag nests in huge colonies on sheltered coastal ledges or among rocks. The helpless young are more likely to survive where there are large numbers of adults to drive away attackers. The nest is made of a pile of seaweed, which is stuck together with the birds' droppings, called guano.

Jagged, hooked bill for grasping slippery fish firmly.

Imperial shag
(Phalacrocorax atriceps)
Length: 72 cm (2 ft 4 in)

Gentoo penguins and a few imperial shags nest on rocky islands around Antarctica in summer. Female gentoo penguins lay their eggs as soon as the ice and snow melts in spring.

Huge, hooked bill for gobbling up fish or squid.

Large eyes for searching for food out at sea.

During the courtship display the birds face one another, make groaning noises, snap their bills open and shut, and fence with their bills.

Wandering albatross
(Diomedea exulans)
Wingspan: 3.6 m (11 ft 10 in)

WANDERING ALBATROSS

This magnificent albatross has the largest wingspan of any bird alive today. On its long, narrow wings, it glides effortlessly over the southern oceans at great speed, using air currents rising off the waves to lift it up into the air. It comes to the Antarctic islands only to nest. The chicks stay in the nest for almost a year before they grow all their feathers for flying. The parents feed out at sea, then cough up some of this food for the chicks to eat. Both adults and young can spray the sticky, smelly, oily food mixture up to 2 m (6 ft) to drive away enemies, such as great skuas.

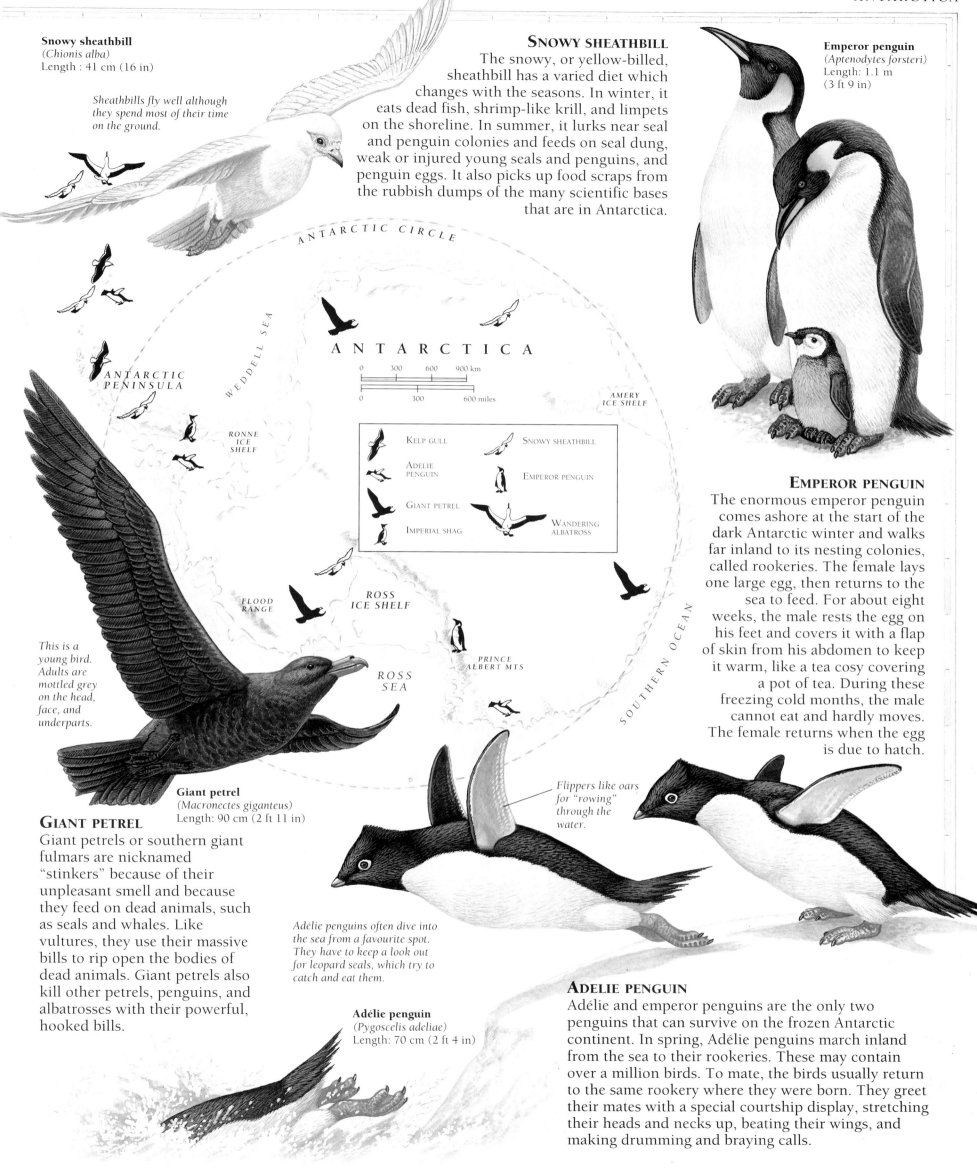

Snowy sheathbill
(*Chionis alba*)
Length : 41 cm (16 in)

Sheathbills fly well although they spend most of their time on the ground.

SNOWY SHEATHBILL

The snowy, or yellow-billed, sheathbill has a varied diet which changes with the seasons. In winter, it eats dead fish, shrimp-like krill, and limpets on the shoreline. In summer, it lurks near seal and penguin colonies and feeds on seal dung, weak or injured young seals and penguins, and penguin eggs. It also picks up food scraps from the rubbish dumps of the many scientific bases that are in Antarctica.

Emperor penguin
(*Aptenodytes forsteri*)
Length: 1.1 m
(3 ft 9 in)

ANTARCTIC CIRCLE

WEDDELL SEA

ANTARCTIC PENINSULA

ANTARCTICA

0   300   600   900 km

0   300   600 miles

AMERY ICE SHELF

RONNE ICE SHELF

KELP GULL		SNOWY SHEATHBILL	
ADELIE PENGUIN		EMPEROR PENGUIN	
GIANT PETREL		WANDERING ALBATROSS	
IMPERIAL SHAG			

FLOOD RANGE

ROSS ICE SHELF

ROSS SEA

PRINCE ALBERT MTS

SOUTHERN OCEAN

EMPEROR PENGUIN

The enormous emperor penguin comes ashore at the start of the dark Antarctic winter and walks far inland to its nesting colonies, called rookeries. The female lays one large egg, then returns to the sea to feed. For about eight weeks, the male rests the egg on his feet and covers it with a flap of skin from his abdomen to keep it warm, like a tea cosy covering a pot of tea. During these freezing cold months, the male cannot eat and hardly moves. The female returns when the egg is due to hatch.

This is a young bird. Adults are mottled grey on the head, face, and underparts.

Giant petrel
(*Macronectes giganteus*)
Length: 90 cm (2 ft 11 in)

GIANT PETREL

Giant petrels or southern giant fulmars are nicknamed "stinkers" because of their unpleasant smell and because they feed on dead animals, such as seals and whales. Like vultures, they use their massive bills to rip open the bodies of dead animals. Giant petrels also kill other petrels, penguins, and albatrosses with their powerful, hooked bills.

Flippers like oars for "rowing" through the water.

Adélie penguins often dive into the sea from a favourite spot. They have to keep a look out for leopard seals, which try to catch and eat them.

Adélie penguin
(*Pygoscelis adeliae*)
Length: 70 cm (2 ft 4 in)

ADELIE PENGUIN

Adélie and emperor penguins are the only two penguins that can survive on the frozen Antarctic continent. In spring, Adélie penguins march inland from the sea to their rookeries. These may contain over a million birds. To mate, the birds usually return to the same rookery where they were born. They greet their mates with a special courtship display, stretching their heads and necks up, beating their wings, and making drumming and braying calls.

Travellers of the World

EVERY YEAR NEARLY HALF of all the birds in the world set off on journeys to find food, water, more space, or to avoid bad weather. These regular journeys are called migration, from the Latin word *migrare*, meaning to go from one place to another. Migration usually takes place at night, but some birds, such as swallows, migrate during the day. Migration journeys are often very dangerous for birds and millions never reach their destinations. They may run out of energy or be unable to find enough food to keep going. Many migrants are also killed by bad weather or by people and other predators lying in wait along traditional routes.

WORLD MIGRATION ROUTES

This map shows the main routes or "flyways" that birds follow on migration (although birds generally move over a wide area rather than a narrow path and they may switch from one flyway to another.)

In North America, two-thirds of all the bird species that spend the summer there travel south for the winter. Another major winter route is from Europe to Africa. Many birds prefer to avoid crossing the Mediterranean Sea because there are no rising air currents to help them soar and glide along. So they cross it at its narrowest points – for example by the Strait of Gibraltar.

The centre of huge continents, such as Asia, are good places for birds to feed and nest in spring and summer, but they get very cold in winter. So many birds migrate from the heart of Asia to the coasts.

SETTING OUT

Before migration, birds eat as much as they can to build up fat reserves in their bodies and give them enough energy to keep going. They usually grow new feathers for the journey too. Birds know when to migrate because of changes in the weather and also because of a biological "clock" in their brain which responds to changes in daylight hours. As the days get shorter in autumn, birds such as these barn swallows, become restless, and get ready to set off by gathering in flocks.

As they migrate, the swallows feed on flying insects to keep up their strength.

Barn swallow
(Hirundo rustica)

Swallows have long, pointed wings for fast and powerful flight. It takes them five or six weeks to fly from Europe to Africa.

FINDING THE WAY

There is still a lot we do not understand about how birds find their way, or navigate, on migration. They seem to know instinctively which way to go because many young birds make migration journeys for the first time without the help of adults.

Birds also steer by the Sun, the Moon, and stars, and the Earth's magnetic field. A few birds, such as shearwaters and petrels, pick up scents carried by the wind and use these to navigate their way across open oceans. Birds that migrate by day probably find their way year after year by following familiar landmarks, such as river valleys, mountain ranges, and coastlines.

FINDING OUT ABOUT MIGRATION

To learn how far birds migrate and where they go, scientists put metal or plastic rings on their legs. The rings are numbered or colour-coded and have an address on them. It is then possible to identify individual birds and keep records of their migration movements. Another way of tracking birds' movements over shorter distances is by using a radio collar, like the one this short-eared owl is wearing.

Short-tailed shearwater
(Puffinus tenuirostris)

This shearwater nests in Tasmania, in Australia, and on islands in the South Pacific Ocean. In April, it flies north to Japan and east to the United States, before heading south again for the winter.

THE JOURNEY

Birds use a lot of energy for continuous flapping flight so on long journeys they have to try and conserve their strength. Some, such as these common cranes, fly in a V-formation so that the birds following the leader do not use up as much energy pushing aside the air as they fly. Others, such as white storks, make use of rising hot air currents – called thermals – to glide and soar without using up any energy. Seabirds glide on currents rising off the ocean waves. A few birds can build up enough stores of body fat to fly non-stop for four days; others have to stop and feed every day.

Common cranes migrate by day and by night from Europe to Africa. They are strong fliers and can cross the Mediterranean at its widest point.

Common crane
(Grus grus)

Birds often migrate in flocks of thousands of birds. Flying in a V-formation helps these common cranes to save energy on a long journey.

MIGRATION FROM NORTH TO SOUTH

In the northern hemisphere, where much of the land is covered with ice and snow in winter, many birds, including the American golden plover, migrate. They spend summer in the north and fly south to warmer places for the winter, returning north again in spring.

Very few landbirds migrate in the opposite direction – from the southern to the northern hemisphere. But several southern seabirds, such as the short-tailed shearwater, do migrate over the Equator to the oceans of the northern hemisphere for the summer because the climate is warmer and there is more food there.

American golden plover
(Pluvialis dominica)

The golden plover nests in the tundra of Alaska and northern Canada and migrates down to the pampas of South America to spend the winter there.

AMAZING MIGRANTS

Arctic tern
(Sterna paradisaea)

Champion migrant
Every year, the Arctic tern flies from the top to the bottom of the world and back – a distance of about 36,000 km (22,000 miles).

High fliers
Most birds fly below 91 m (300 ft) on migration but some cross high mountains. Condors migrate at 6,035 m (19,800 ft) in the Andes, and geese in the Himalayas migrate at heights of more than 9,500 m (31,168 ft).

Weight-watcher
Small birds, such as the blackpoll warbler, may double their weight before migrating in order to "fuel" their journey.

Tiny migrant
Most hummingbirds do not migrate far, but the ruby-throated hummingbird travels up to 3,200 km (2,000 miles) across the eastern USA and the Gulf of Mexico to Central America. Experts do not know how such tiny birds have the energy for such a long flight.

Ruby-throated hummingbird
(Archilochus colubris)

Birds in Danger

BIRDS ARE ENDANGERED ALL OVER the world. More than 1,000 bird species, more than 10 per cent of all known birds, are in danger of dying out. The parrot family is the most threatened group, with over 70 species at risk. Many birds die out naturally as a result of changes in the environment and new species develop to take their place. But people have speeded up this extinction process. They have increased the number of threats to bird survival by destroying habitats, causing pollution, hunting birds, and catching them to keep in cages. We urgently need to do more to help save the world's rare birds.

THREATENED BIRDS

These are some of the rarest birds in the world. In most cases there are less than 150 of each species left in the wild, although people are trying to save them in nature reserves or protected areas.

Eskimo curlew
(*Numenius borealis*)
Americas.

Ivory-billed woodpecker
(*Campephilus principalis*)
Americas

Chatham Island black robin
(*Petroica traversi*)
New Zealand

Noisy scrub bird
(*Atrichornis clamosus*)
Australia

Gurney's pitta
(*Pitta gurneyi*)
Thailand

White-tailed sea eagle
(*Haliaeetus albicilla*)
Europe

HABITAT DESTRUCTION

Dalmatian pelican
(*Pelecanus crispus*)

This is by far the most serious threat to bird life today. About two-thirds of the endangered birds in the world are threatened by the destruction of their habitat. Marshes and swamps have been drained and used for farms; grasslands have been ploughed up to grow crops or graze cattle; and forests have been cleared for their timber or to make way for farms, houses, and mines. For example, dalmatian pelicans (above) were once common in southeastern Europe, the Russian Federation, Iran, and Turkey. They have now become an endangered species due to disturbance from people, and drainage of the rivers, lakes, deltas, and estuaries on which they nest. Rainforests are one of the richest habitats for birds, but more than half of the world's rainforests have already been destroyed and an area of rainforest about the size of a soccer pitch disappears every second.

HUNTING AND COLLECTING

Until about 60 years ago, many birds were hunted to obtain feathers, such as ostrich plumes, to decorate hats for the fashion trade. Millions of birds such as egrets were killed each year for their beautiful courtship plumes. In the past people have also significantly reduced bird numbers by hunting them and collecting their eggs for food. For example, passenger pigeons were once the most abundant birds in the world. Huge flocks used to darken the skies. Yet in the 19th century, Europeans setting up home in North America killed millions of them. In less than 100 years, the passenger pigeon was extinct. Hunting birds for food is not as important today, but people still hunt birds for sport, especially waterbirds such as ducks and geese. Birds that follow the same routes on migration are easy targets for predators, including people.

Many of Asia's tropical rainforests have been cleared. This causes a great threat to Asian bird life. The Japanese crested ibis, for example, almost died out due to destruction of its forest home and is now a protected species.

Crested ibis
(*Nipponia nippon*)

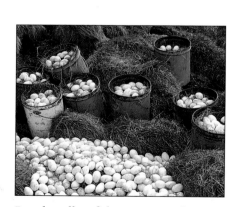

People collect fulmar eggs in their thousands from breeding colonies off the coasts of Iceland. This need not threaten bird numbers as long as the amount of eggs taken is not too high.

Houbara bustard
(*Chlamydotis undulata*)

The houbara bustard of Pakistan became rare because it was hunted and killed for sport.

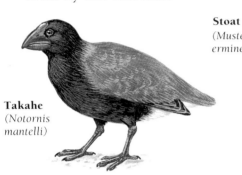

Black paradise flycatcher
(Tersiphone corvina)

INTRODUCED SPECIES

As people have moved from place to place, they have taken with them a variety of animals, especially cats, rats, dogs, and birds, such as house sparrows. Introduced species cause particular problems on islands, such as Hawaii and New Zealand, where the native birds often have no defence against the new intruders. They attack the birds already living in a place, spread disease, and compete with them for food and space. Introduced species can also rapidly change the habitat of their new homes. The native birds cannot usually adapt to these rapid changes and soon die out. For example, black paradise flycatchers (above) were once found in large numbers throughout the Seychelles, but they are now found mainly on one island and there are fewer than 100 left. They were driven out of other areas by rats and cats.

Takahe
(Notornis mantelli)

Stoat
(Mustela erminea)

Stoats were introduced into New Zealand to try to control the rising numbers of rats and other small mammals. Unfortunately, they raided the eggs and chicks of the takahe, a rare flightless bird, and it almost became extinct as a result.

THE END OF THE LINE

Some birds have died out completely. One example is the dusky seaside sparrow. Until the 1940s, thousands of these small songbirds lived on the saltmarshes on the east coast of Florida, in the United States. Then in the mid-1950s, Cape Canaveral and the NASA Space Centre were built on these marshes and dykes were constructed to stop the tidal flooding. The sparrows needed the floodwaters to provide food for their survival, so they soon began to die out. Some birds were protected in a wildlife refuge, but in 1975, fire destroyed their habitat and no females have been seen since. The last 100 per cent dusky seaside sparrow died in 1989.

Dusky seaside sparrow
(Ammodramus maritimus nigrescens)

TRADE IN CAGED BIRDS

Many people like to keep birds in cages as pets for their colour, their songs, and their company. Most of these birds are taken from Africa, Asia, and South America and bought by people in western countries. Small, seed-eating songbirds make up about 80 per cent of the trade, but about 600,000 parrots are also traded each year. Parrots fetch much higher prices than songbirds.

Caged songbird

The worst part of the trade is the large number of birds that die during capture, while waiting to be sold, or on their journey to a life in captivity. They are often tightly packed in boxes without food or water for their journey. Out of every 10 birds caught in the wild, only about one ever reaches a pet shop.

POLLUTION

Birds are threatened by all sorts of chemicals that pollute the air, land, or water – from oil and acid rain, to pesticides and factory wastes. Oil spills at sea occur after shipping accidents or when tankers illegally wash out their tanks. The oil causes great damage to seabirds. It makes their feathers stick together so they can no longer keep out the cold or wet and it prevents them from diving for food. The birds may also be poisoned by swallowing the oil when they preen their feathers. When birds such as this jackass penguin (above), are caught in an oil spill, they have to be cleaned very swiftly otherwise they die from cold and hunger.

Acid rain, caused when chemicals from vehicle exhaust fumes and power stations mix with water in the air, is also a problem for birds. The rain falls on forests and lakes, damaging or killing the waterbirds or the food they eat.

WHAT WE CAN DO TO HELP

The world's rare birds need our help if they are to survive. Birds are closely linked to all the other wildlife on the planet, so if there are problems for birds, these serve as a warning of problems for plants, animals, and people. We can help by doing the following:

Mauritius pink pigeon
(Nesoenas mayeri)

- Set aside areas of land and water as nature reserves or wildlife sanctuaries where birds will be protected from disturbance, hunting, and introduced species.

- Set up more artificial feeding areas for birds to help them survive in harsh climates. The machine shown below distributes food for trumpeter swans in North America during the winter. This keeps them alive when lakes, where they usually feed on water plants, freeze over.

- Breed rare birds in captivity and release them back into the wild. Numbers of the Mauritius pink pigeon were built up in this way.

- Ban the hunting of rare species and stop birds being shot on migration.

- Stop keeping wild birds in cages and use birds bred in captivity instead.

- Reduce the amount of pollution, especially from oil spills and pesticides.

- Carry out research to find out as much as possible about how birds live, so we can plan the best ways to conserve them.

- Pass international laws to protect endangered species.

- Join conservation organizations to protest, raise money, and make other people aware of the problems.

INDEX

ACKNOWLEDGEMENTS

Dorling Kindersley would like to thank the following: David Gillingwater, Rachael Foster, and Mark Thompson for design assistance, and Lynn Bresler for compiling the index.

Picture research Clive Webster

Maps Andrew MacDonald

Globes and diagrams John Hutchinson

Cartographic consultant Roger Bullen

Bird symbols Heather Blackham

Photo credits
a=above, b=below, c=centre, l=left, r=right, t=top
Bridgeman Art Library: 24cl.
Bruce Coleman: 53bc.
Erwin and Peggy Bauer 16bc Alain Compost 62bl;
Gerald Cubitt 37tr, 41tl, 43tc, 47tc, 63c;
Peter Davey 39tl; Christer Fredriksson 35tc;
Jeff Foot Productions 11tc, 63bc;
Michael Freeman 21cl; Frances Furlong 50br;
Giorgio Gualgo 25bl; Pekka Helo 28c;
Joy Langsbury 17c; Wayne Lankinen 11tl;
L C Marigo 23c; Fco Marquez 30tc;
Dieter and Mary Plage 45br; G D Plage 45tl;

Fritz Prenzel 51tr; Hans Reinhard 54tr;
Gary Retherford 19bl; Leonard Lee Rue 58cl;
John Shaw 9tr, 12c; Kim Taylor 33c;
Norman Owen Tomalin 26bc; Nicholas de Vore 43tl;
G Ziesler 22bc.
The Image Bank: 7tl;
James Carmichael 20br; Per Eide 27tl;
Don King 42cr; Peter Muller 27tc.
Frank Lane: C Carvalho 35tr; Tom and Pam Gardner
52c; A R Hamblin 18bl; Eric and David Hosking 35tl;
40br; S Jonasson 62bc; S Maslowski 13tc; R van
Nostrand 15tr; F Polking 24tr; P Reynolds 61tl;
L Robinson 55bl; J Wisniewski 36br;

NHPA: Anthony Bannister 38br, 39c;
V Garcia Canseco 31cr; B Chudleigh 57tl;
J S Gifford 32cl; Melvin Grey 33cr;
Stephen Krasemann 14cr;
Orion Press 49tc; Otto Rogge 50bl, 57cr;
Morten Strange 47cr;
Roger Tidman 29cr.
Oxford Scientific Films:
Kjell Sandved 10br.
Planet Earth Pictures / John Waters /
Bernadette Spiegel 7c.
South American Pictures: 11tr.

ld be returned by the last date entered below

593.4